BK,

HERE YOU GO - I HOPE YOU enjoy READING it AS MUCH I DID writing it -

ALL the best for the KLEIN Camp

Your friend

Charley

Magic in the Dark

MAGIC IN THE DARK

One Family's Century of Adventures in Cinema

CHARLES B. MOSS JR. & JONATHAN KAY

sh.

SUTHERLAND
HOUSE

TORONTO, 2021

Sutherland House
416 Moore Ave., Suite 205
Toronto, ON M4G 1C9

First hardcover edition, December 2021

If you are interested in inviting one of our authors to a live event or
media appearance, please contact publicity@sutherlandhousebooks.com
and visit our website at sutherlandhousebooks.com for more
information about our authors and their schedules.

Printed in the United States
Cover designed by Lena Yang
Book composed by Karl Hunt

Library and Archives Canada Cataloguing in Publication
Title: Magic in the dark : one family's century of adventures in cinema /
Charles B. Moss Jr. and Jonathan Kay.
Names: Moss, Charles B., Jr., 1944- author. | Kay, Jonathan, 1968- author.
Description: Includes index.
Identifiers: Canadiana 20210219300 | ISBN 9781989555484 (hardcover)
Subjects: LCSH: Moss, B. S., 1878-1951—Family. | LCSH: Moss family. |
LCSH: B.S. Moss Enterprises—History. | LCSH: Bow Tie Cinemas—History. |
LCSH: Motion picture theater owners—United States—Biography. |
LCSH: Motion picture theaters—United States—History. |
LCSH: Motion picture industry—United States—History. |
LCGFT: Biographies.
Classification: LCC PN1998.2 .M67 2021 |
DDC 791.43092/273—dc23

ISBN 978-1-989555-48-4

TO B.S., BUSTER,
AND THE PRESENT AND FUTURE
GENERATIONS OF MY FAMILY.

—Charley Moss Jr., New York, 2021

CONTENTS

INTRODUCTION

The "Boring" Part

CHARLES ("CHARLEY") B. MOSS, JR. is in an Uber on his way to his favorite bookstore, Book Soup, on West Hollywood's Sunset Strip. The car is driven by one of the many creative men and women who still migrate to L.A. in search of fame and fortune, this fellow a graffiti artist who rents out galleries to put on art exhibits, among other side hustles. He shows Charley the tattoos on his hands, representing the initials of his last serious girlfriend. He tells a funny and sad story about how the relationship ended three weeks after the ink was complete and how he couldn't afford to get the tattoos removed. Then the conversation turns to Charley. What does he do for a living?

"Oh, I'm in film," Charley says, giving his usual vague, deflective response to such questions.

"What part of the industry?" the driver asks. This is L.A., after all, where even your Uber driver knows the difference between associate and assistant producer.

"The boring part," Charley answers, again by reflex. "I run a chain of movie theaters." He steers the conversation back to tattoos.

Out of the car and challenged on why he would describe as "boring" an industry that has fascinated him for more than four decades, Charley confesses that he deliberately downplays his industry and his own role in it when the subject arises in casual conversation. People hear the word "film," he says, and they think Hollywood, and expect a certain kind of perspective, a certain kind of anecdote.

He's correct, of course. The evidence is right there in Book Soup, which devotes much of its shelf space to books on film. The section on film history alone contains hundreds of well-known titles, many of them about the small group of mostly (not exclusively) Jewish men who, like Charley's grandfather, B.S. Moss, fled to the United States from Europe in the latter years of the nineteenth century.

Read the biographies of moguls such as Samuel Goldwyn, Carl Laemmle, Adolph Zukor, Louis B. Mayer, William Fox, and the Warner brothers, and you'll recognize the B.S. Moss type. Neil Gabler captured some of the characteristics in his 1988 classic, *An Empire Of Their Own: How The Jews Invented Hollywood*: "Having come primarily from fashion and retail, they understood public taste and were masters at gauging market swings, at merchandising, at pirating away customers and beating the competition . . . As immigrants themselves, they had a peculiar sensitivity to the dreams and aspirations of other immigrants and working-class families, two overlapping groups that made up a significant portion of the early movie-going audience."

B.S. Moss also was part of the larger, enduring cultural project that these men crowdsourced: the creation of a mythical, cinematic, hyper-patriotic America "where fathers were strong, families stable, people attractive, resilient, resourceful and decent . . . a 'shadow' America [that] idealized every old glorifying bromide about the country."

But, in other ways, the giants of early Hollywood chronicled by Gabler and others were very different from B.S. Moss, even if they were born during the same period and worked in the same industry. Many of the Jewish "emperors" of Hollywood were troubled, controlling, self-destructive men with complicated backstories and turbulent domestic lives. English, in many cases, was not their first language, and they could be ill at ease and insecure in polite society, having grown up amid destitution. "He talks the English he learned on the fur bench," is how one contemporary described Zukor. They often treated their own relatives poorly, even cruelly, and acted tyrannically within the entities they created. As with many alpha figures who rule by decree, they were unable to build stable organizations that survived their retirements, let alone found family dynasties.

B.S. Moss, by contrast, exhibited the understated confidence and refined manners of an establishment business figure. Peruse the Moss family archives and the many newspaper articles about B.S. and you won't find anything that describes him as less than a gentleman. In his business dealings, he struck those who knew him as unusually earnest and meticulous. He was an honorable father and husband and a committed patriot who, during the early 1940s, used his theaters to support the war effort. The New York City theaters he built and ran had names such as the Hamilton and the Jefferson, which evoked the history and character of his adopted country. He was active in charity work and led trade groups that encouraged movie exhibitors to pursue high aesthetic and moral standards. It's an old cliché, the "model immigrant," but it fit B.S. Moss.

Perhaps it is no coincidence that more tempestuous men such as Fox (who went to prison in the early 1940s for bribing a judge) would have their names embedded in entertainment history for their role in making films, while a less flamboyant figure such as B.S. Moss would create and operate the theaters where audiences would watch them. Hollywood, lest we forget, was quite literally part of the Wild West, having taken seed in the Vine Street barn where Cecil B. DeMille and Oscar Apfel filmed *The Squaw Man* in 1913. Crazy things could, and did, happen on a film set. It was a place where tortured geniuses had their tantrums and drank themselves blind out of the sight and earshot of respectable society. Fortunes were won on one film, lost on another. Stars, born in an instant, flamed out just as quickly, often in dissolution or disgrace. Then, as now, the world of film production offered outsized risks and rewards, and attracted personalities to match.

B.S. Moss knew this world well, having served as producer for numerous silent films, including the melodrama *Break The News To Mother* (advertised as "a timely select special of tender sentiment, undying faith, and mother love") and *Birth Control*, a ground-breaking 1917 documentary that became the first film ever banned under an infamous 1915 U.S. Supreme Court ruling that permitted the censorship of movies. But once he launched his first chain of theaters (a "circuit," to use the still-current industry term), he entered a different world. Then, as now, an exhibitor's business operations are rooted in communities, in brick and mortar. They are judged daily in the same unforgiving way a customer judges a restaurant or a retail store. A studio can follow a hit with a bomb season after season and still balance the books. But a customer who gets bad service at a theater may never come back.

Every generation of Mosses came to the movie business in its own way. B.S. Moss was a silent-film producer before he began running movie houses. His son, and Charley's father, took a turn producing the 1950s television shows. He would join the family's exhibition business in its golden years, the middle decades of the twentieth century when the Moss-run Criterion Theatre on Broadway, opened in 1936, was often was the only place in the whole country where Americans could attend the premiere showing of a blockbuster film.

These openings were major cultural events, attracting film stars alongside fawning crowds large enough to paralyze the local road network, with B.S. Moss and his son taking in a storm of photographers' flashbulbs as celebrities in their own right. On November 8, 1956 the Criterion was the only place you could see *The Ten Commandments*; the same with *Lawrence of Arabia* on December 15, 1962, and *South Pacific* on March 19, 1958. On October 21, 1964 patrons paid $150 apiece to see the premiere of *My Fair Lady* (with Charley's father directing profits to The Will Rogers Hospital and Research Laboratory), a film that kept running continuously at the Criterion for a year and a half. Even after the premier, it was the only place showing *My Fair Lady* within an hour's drive.

These arrangements are difficult to imagine in today's era, when movies open at thousands of theaters around the world simultaneously and then disappear after a few weeks into their Netflix and Amazon Prime afterlives. But this was a time before the multiplex, and a single Times Square theater often would have monopoly exhibition rights for the entire metro region. While Hollywood controlled how movies were made, it was midtown Manhattan that often set the terms for how they'd be unveiled.

One of Charley Moss's early experiences in show business was finding extras for scenes in *Love Story* while a law student in Boston. After a brief career as a producer of low-budget horror movies, he took over from his father, operating out of the same Criterion Theatre building at the heart of Times Square, in third- and fourth-floor offices now sitting atop flagship locations for The Gap, Old Navy, Starbucks and McDonalds. The Moss family collectively decided to name it the Bow Tie Building in honor of Charles' trademark fashion accessory—and for the distinctive bowtie shape formed by the intersection of Broadway and 7th Avenue at West Forty-Fifth Street, where the building sits.

New York City, and more particularly Times Square, with its long and storied history, is one of the characters in this book. B.S. Moss came to Times Square in its glory days, the age of Cole Porter and Damon Runyon. His grandson, Charley, entered the business when Times Square was at its nadir and the people who inhabited it played by a thinner rulebook. He can recall face-to-face meetings with a projectionists' union representative who started negotiations by casually displaying his handgun. A couple of tenants who operated a discotheque in the Moss family building were sent to jail on tax charges when it was discovered they were running no fewer than four sets of books. A neighboring Times Square property owner decided to demolish a row of adjoining flophouse hotels in the dead of night, without benefit of a permit or, more importantly, bothering to turn off the power or gas feed. The Moss family saga might have ended right then in a ball of flame. Life is more secure, if less colorful, in the Disneyfied era of Times Square.

What has never wavered over the years is the spirit of professional self-effacement that characterizes each generation of the Moss family, and the entire film-exhibition industry of which they've been a part. In the film section of Book Soup, for instance, the shelves groan with books on the art of acting, compendiums of all-time great movies and biographies of legendary directors. The few books that relate at all to the business of film exhibition tend to be trade-targeted resources such as Jason Squire's *The Movie Business Book*, or dense academic treatises such as Douglas Gomery's *Shared Pleasures: A History of Movie Presentation in the United States*, or coffee-table books that focus on the architectural details of vintage movie houses. The legacies of B.S. and all the other exhibitors who've played a vital but less glamorous role on the retail side of the industry have been passed over, notwithstanding our culture's deep interest in film and the fact that there would have been no movies without movie houses.

Charley's own favorite book about his industry isn't a work of history, but a two-decade-old novel by Elizabeth McCracken entitled *Niagara Falls All Over Again*. The book tells the story of two comedians—the refined, tragically self-aware straight man Mose Sharp, and his self-destructive, flamboyantly comedic man-child partner, Rocky Carter. Charley loves the story not only because it traces the arc of his grandfather's career—from vaudeville to film—but because it captures the yin and yang of professional life in his movie industry. Ultimately, every mogul needs a Moss, just as every Carter needs a Sharp.

This book is not intended as an exhaustive and definitive history of film exhibition, let alone the movie industry. Nor is it a straightforward biographical treatment of the Moss family and its role in film exhibition— even if their lives provide a natural structure for the story that spools out in the coming chapters. Rather, this is a book about the changing face of the entertainment industry and America itself, as seen from the inside of a birdcage ticket booth.

For all the many forms of competition that theaters now face in an entertainment-packed world, movie-going is one of the few rituals that, in its bare essentials, really hasn't changed much over the last century. People are happy to pay to watch first-rate filmed entertainment in a crowded theater. That consistency has allowed Charley, a third generation Moss (working closely with a fourth, his son Ben) to look back on the last twelve decades of his family tradition as a single unbroken story since his grandfather arrived from Galicia as a child.

At the same time, much has changed. The audiences, their neighborhoods, the theater buildings, the projection technology, the theater staff, the content of the films, and the terms on which they are exhibited—it has all been in constant flux. In this respect, the exhibition business is like any other: you either adapt to changing tastes and trends, or you get pushed out by others who do. Its commitment to keeping pace has led the Moss family from Nickelodeons and vaudeville emporiums to talkies and blockbusters and the multiplex. Its business has survived because, more often than not, it has been ahead of market trends. It is one of precious few family businesses to resist the corporatization of the American entertainment industry. As such, it's an American success story, one that holds important lessons about how a multi-generational business can continually re-invent itself and its product while staying true to its original values. And there's nothing "boring" about it.

CHAPTER ONE

It All Started With These Guys

VISIT A FABRIC SHOP, or surf the fashion offerings on eBay, and you will stumble upon a product called sponged wool. The term has become obscure in modern times, but in the late nineteenth-century sponged wool was in great demand, and the sponging process had a big role in the clothing business. New York City's garment industry, dominating a large swath of Manhattan from the Bowery up to the southern edge of Central Park and across the breadth of the island between Fourteenth and Thirty-Fourth Streets, alone employed thousands of cloth spongers.

A sponger's job was to pre-shrink fabric through the application of steam. As with many positions in the garment trade, manual sponging was hard, menial labor that required real skill. But New York was teeming with newly arrived European immigrants willing to accept low wages for steady employment. A typical sponger in the 1890s earned as little as eight dollars for six long days a week, sweating in clouds of steam and puddles of stagnant water, cheek-by-jowl with other laborers. The shop floors were ready incubators for every imaginable kind of germ (tuberculosis—the "tailor's disease"—was especially feared.) Until the deaths of 146 garment workers in New York's infamous Triangle Shirtwaist Factory fire of 1911, workplace-safety laws were almost non-existent and child labor was common. To be a cloth sponger was to spend one's days dreaming of a better life.

One especially successful dreamer was a young New York City sponger named Benjamin Moss, who quit his job in 1900 after his boss refused to raise his pay. Together with a fellow sponger named William Fox, Moss set up a fabric-supply company called Knickerbocker Cloth Examining and Shrinking, just south of Washington Square Park.

At the time, neither man seemed destined for greatness. Their new business suffered a series of disasters from the get-go. In one particularly dangerous incident, Fox and Moss confronted a Knickerbocker sales agent who'd borrowed twenty-five dollars from their company under false pretenses. The agent, one Nathan May, had claimed he needed to treat his sick child; in fact, he was financing an affair with his mistress. In the ensuing fracas, the salesman pulled out a gun and put a bullet through the brim of Moss's hat before killing himself in front of police and horrified witnesses.

Shortly thereafter, Fox and Moss went their separate ways. In 1902, Fox opened a slot-machine arcade in Brooklyn. He also bought one of New York City's first nickelodeons and started a film-production company, which he named after himself. From there he expanded into many branches of the film industry, eventually making an international name for himself by producing movies. He fell on hard times in the Great Depression and lost control of his company, Fox Films, but his name would live on at Twentieth Century Fox.

His fellow cloth sponger, Benjamin Moss, also put down stakes in the entertainment field and lent his name to an enduring corporate empire, but his career would follow a different path and produce a much different and in important ways more impressive legacy.

B. S. Moss had been born Bernhard Moskowitz in 1875 to Albert and Rose Moskowitz, residents of what is now the Polish town of Wisnicz. Five years later, Albert, a tailor, sailed to New York to start a new life, sending for his family when he was confident he could house and support them. Rose, Bernhard and three other Moss children crossed the Atlantic on a Hamburg America steamship, sailing into port on July 28, 1881, a few months before Bernhard's sixth birthday. As was customary at the time, family members adopted shorter, Americanized names. Bernhard became Benjamin. Moskowitz became Moss.

Albert's three older brothers had already established themselves in New York's textile business. Settling the family in a heavily German area known as Yorkville on Manhattan's Upper East Side, Albert seems soon to have been afflicted by a debilitating psychiatric condition. His listed address on both the 1910 and 1920 censuses was Manhattan State Hospital (then referred to as The New York City Asylum for the Insane), a hulking edifice on Ward's Island that Albert's family members would have been able to see from the Yorkville side of the Harlem River.

On March 3, 1922, the day after Rose's death from colon cancer, Albert was transferred to private care at the more upscale Fair Oaks Sanatorium in Summit, New Jersey, a facility dedicated to the "treatment of all forms of nervous diseases and selected treatment of drug and alcohol addiction." He would spend the last eleven years of his life there. (Family lore casts Rose as a beloved matriarch, but also a penny-pincher, as suggested by the timing of Albert's transfer to Fair Oaks only upon her death.)

It made sense for Rose to pinch pennies. The young family had little on its arrival in America. Benjamin took odd jobs from a young age to support his mother and five younger siblings. An early profile of Moss published in a Jewish magazine notes that he sold newspapers on the streets of New York as a child, even throughout the Great Blizzard of March 1888 which dumped twenty-two inches of snow on the city and chased away other vendors, allowing the gleeful Moss to sell his own copies for the windfall price of twenty-five cents apiece. Benjamin was enrolled for a time in New York's public-school system but eventually dropped out for the good of his family, finding find full-time employment with sponged wool.

B.S. Moss (no one called him Benjamin) was in his mid-twenties when he and William Fox broke out on their own to found Knickerbocker Cloth Examining and Shrinking. The name they chose is significant. It was thoroughly American.

Many of the early Jewish entertainment-industry titans had mixed feelings about their faith, and some shed it entirely. (At least one of the Jewish, Lithuanian-born Shubert brothers who dominated the Times Square theater industry for half a century would become a notorious anti-Semite.) When it came to the actual content of their productions, especially, Hollywood's Jewish "emperors" scrupulously avoided themes or influences that might raise eyebrows among gentiles. Even Jewish actors were looked at askance. As Gould notes, Columbia Pictures co-founder Harry Cohn once "refused to sign a Jewish actor for an important part, saying, 'Around this studio, the only Jews we put in pictures play Indians.'"

B.S. Moss was not a particularly observant Jew. He certainly did not dress in a recognizable Jewish style, and his social life appears to have revolved more around the Friars Club than the synagogue. Moreover, his surviving business ledgers indicate that he at least occasionally worked on Saturday, the Jewish sabbath. But there isn't any evidence to suggest that Moss took steps to disguise or reject his Jewish heritage.

Rather, he married Estelle "Stella" Dreyfus, a woman whose family came with its own fascinating backstory. Stella's father was a Bavarian-born Jewish cowboy who delivered cattle to New York's processing plants in the mid-nineteenth century. B.S. would also take a leadership position in the United Krakauer Aid Society, a charity that helped integrate new Jewish arrivals (such as Moss's own family once had been), and used his professional connections to stage benefit performances on its behalf. A strong-willed woman, Stella hailed from Kingston, New York, and was very proud of her French roots.

Integration, perhaps, was the key. B.S.'s primary sense of identity was rooted in American citizenship. He was a full convert to the American way of life, including its religion of self-improvement. As a young man, he would write down words to upgrade his vocabulary and speak like a proper American. He would expound earnestly of America's history and civic traditions, and collect signatures of former presidents, later naming his first theaters after four founding fathers—Jefferson, Washington, Hamilton, and Franklin.

B.S. Moss's transition from the cloth trades to entertainment was unusually tentative. The careers of storied moviemakers such as Goldwyn and Zukor are marked by eureka moments—either real or mythologized—whereupon the young moguls are seized with the realization of how big the entertainment business could become. Moss hung onto his more mundane cloth-treatment business interests as he made his first investments in entertainment, and he would not fully divest of them until later in life. His caution was warranted. The nickelodeon business into which his former partner William Fox had plunged in 1902 was a new and unproven branch of a fast-growing but ever-changing market for filmed entertainment. The technology, the films, and the methods of exhibition had already seen several revolutions.

* * *

Culturally, the foundations of the motion-picture exhibition business were laid during B.S. Moss's childhood years, when phonographs (then newly invented) would be set up in downtown shopping arcades, allowing passersby to pay a few cents to listen to music, theatrical recitations, political speeches or sermons by using individual ear horns. Believing that the commercial possibilities would be greatly expanded if visuals were added, Thomas Edison developed a method for putting photographs on spinning cylinders that could be coordinated with the sound from his phonograph technology. The device, as put into retail operation, was called the Kinetoscope, and required the viewer to stoop down and put his eye over a peephole as film spooled over a light source. One of the very first Kinetoscopes appeared in 1894 at the corner of Broadway and West Twenty-Seventh Street, where an arcade offered "peep shows" for twenty-five cents admission, a high price considering many laborers were making $8 a week.

Edison wrongly imagined that the potential of his invention lay with individual consumers hovering over their own Kinetoscope boxes, each looking at their own private movie shows. His genius was in the sphere of technological invention, not human social habits. And so it was left to others to turn motion pictures into a public spectacle. Nevertheless, Edison was shrewd enough to realize that whatever the medium of delivery, the real industry bottleneck would be the availability of content: he'd observed that consumers quickly bored of filmed vaudeville acts with titles such as *Trained Bears* and *The Gaiety Girls Dancing*.

Over time, the term "peep show" became synonymous with pornography. It turned out that this was the only type of film most people preferred to watch in the isolated way Edison had imagined. Across the Atlantic in 1895, the Lumière brothers famously staged a public viewing of their Cinématographe at Le Salon Indien du Grand Café in Paris. The actual technology was similar to what Edison had produced. Crucially, however, the images were projected sideways, not vertically, and the light's target was a large screen, not a human eyeball. Hundreds, or even thousands of people could watch the same movie at once, and film became a social experience. Edison knew a good thing when he saw it, and quickly adapted the concept into his next major product, which he called the Vitascope.

The Lumière brothers thought seriously about the possibilities of this new medium, not just a tool to record and re-monetize stage entertainment, but as a vehicle for both art and journalism. Even the inaugural set of short films (each forty-odd seconds long) they showed at Grand Café illustrated the way film could transform mundane forms of human behavior—a baby having breakfast, workers leaving a factory, a random street scene in the city of Lyon—into compelling and thought-provoking vignettes.

The development of film technology did not kill immediately kill vaudeville, the most popular form of American live entertainment at the turn of the twentieth century. Rather, during the early years of film, popular vaudeville theaters became the main outlet of movie distribution. Short films were swapped in among live orators, singers, puppet shows, trained animals, magicians, comedians, and abbreviated theatrical dramas. The content of the films was rudimentary. They were short and had little in the way of plot. Some were nothing more than vaudeville acts recorded at Edison's West Orange, N.J., studio. They were designed to please men with short attention spans, some sober, some not.

Also exhibiting films in the days before movie theaters were itinerant entrepreneurs who traveled from town to town with projectors. Amusement parks, too, got in on the act. By 1904, visitors could ride on something called The Hale's Tour Car: "passengers" were loaded into a stationary coach which was shaken back and forth by a mechanical apparatus while a film of passing landscape was played on the side. It was an early prototype of the 3-D rides at modern amusement parks.

The first theaters that catered exclusively to film were nickelodeons, which within a few years of William Fox's 1902 investment were sprouting up everywhere in the United States. As with vaudeville, the nickelodeons offered a continuous run of entertainment during the day—typically an hour-long succession of very short films repeated on cycle. Viewers came and went as they pleased after paying their nickel entry fee. The second half of the word nickelodeon originates with the melodion, a small German-style accordion that was popular with folk musicians.

Apart from the melodion or a piano, operators did not invest in atmospherics or creature comforts. They worked out of converted arcades and other low-rent storefront locations, often adjoined dance halls and saloons catering to immigrants and tenement-dwellers. "The auditorium, typically the only room inside, was little more than a converted screening room, long and narrow and darkly lit, even when patrons were streaming in and out," writes Gomery in *Shared Pleasures*. Between fifty and a few hundred customers would perch on benches or cheap chairs and stare at nine-by-twelve-foot screen (often made of bed sheets) on the back wall. A typical nickelodeon could break even if it brought in two hundred dollars, or four thousand customers, every month, or about sixty customers per show cycle.

The nickelodeon's heyday played out in the first decade of the twentieth-century, right in B.S. Moss's backyard. Many of New York's nickelodeons were set up in his childhood neighborhood of Yorkville, or in the Bowery, an area Moss would have known well as a hub for clothing production, and in the Jewish parts of Brooklyn where William Fox had first set up shop. New York City was at the center of America's nascent movie business.

* * *

As mentioned in the last chapter, cloth-sponging and entertainment were not as unrelated as one might imagine. Until the emergence of anti-competitive film trusts, both fields presented few barriers to entry for ambitious men. They required no academic or professional credentials and could be learned from the bottom up. Perhaps most importantly, they rewarded businessmen who maintained a close, everyday connection to the fickle tastes of average consumers. Entrepreneurs who combined local market knowledge with the ability to raise even small amounts of start-up capital could strike out on their own and be successful. In 1906, Carl Laemmle, who'd immigrated from Europe at an early age, opened up his first nickelodeon in a Polish neighborhood of Chicago. Within a decade, he'd founded Universal Pictures, and was running the biggest film-production facility in the world.

By the time B.S. Moss was ready to make his move, there was a well-trod path of young men individually or with their families had fled the miseries of European ghettos to reinvent themselves in America, first in the garment trade or retail, and next in entertainment. They tended to be rough-spun individuals with sharp elbows. "Lewis J. Selznick, who came from a family of eighteen, migrated from Kiev to London at the age of twelve," writes Heywood Gould. "Samuel Goldwyn left Warsaw when he was eleven. Adolph Zukor arrived in England from Hungary at the age of fifteen, with forty dollars sewn in his pockets. The moguls began in the retail trades traditionally followed by Jews. Goldwyn was a glove salesman, Selznick a jeweler, [William] Fox a cloth sponger, Zukor a furrier . . . They were drawn to what was then the nickelodeon business by retailing, not by artistic interests . . . The set-up was ideal: quick turnover, cash customers, and no returns."

The path into entertainment was so attractive that it was soon overcrowded. Competition in the nickelodeon business was fierce. New York had more than a hundred of them and, by one estimate, the United States had as many as ten thousand. Many markets were over-saturated, and some of the most ambitious operations, such as the Vitascope Hall in New Orleans, opened and closed within a few months. A 1907 editorial in *Moving Picture World* lamented the "cutthroat competition between the little nickelodeon owners . . . they are beginning to compete each other out of existence."

The problem was that nickelodeons, like the films they showed, had become a low-brow commodity market. Most women and most people of means wouldn't be caught dead in a nickelodeon. The men who would go on to make great fortunes in the film business were the ones who figured out that the great mass of respectable Americans wanted more than to sit on a bench and be titillated by the gimmicky likes of *The Fete of a Millionaire at Budapest* and *Shooting the Chutes at Geneva*. They wanted to be truly entertained in a setting the whole family could enjoy. That meant better content and better theaters.

The Lumière brothers had taken an important step by realizing that movie exhibition is a social experience: people would prefer to sit with friends or family and watch a movie projected on a wall than stare downwards at the innards of one of Thomas Edison's arcade machines (or, at least, they would until the age of the personal computer and the iPad). The Lumières also sensed the potential of more meaningful content, but making it would not be easy. The early exhibitors were in a chicken-and-egg situation. They couldn't attract a better class of customers without making longer and superior films. Legitimate stage actors, however, refused to risk their good names by appearing in a medium widely regarded as a cheap novelty.

Not surprisingly, then, better theaters emerged before better content, and B.S. Moss was among the leaders. Newly married, but as yet without children, he had money to invest. A surviving set of handwritten ledgers from his Consolidated Cloth Sponging Works, located at the corner of Prince and Lafayette Streets in the neighborhood between the Bowery and Soho now known as Nolita, put his 1903 weekly take-home pay at thirty dollars a week, about four times the average American weekly salary. The ledgers also show that Moss employed eight workers in 1903 and more than thirty by late 1905. Business was good, and whereas most of his earliest employees appear to have been menial or semi-skilled workers earning relatively modest wages, Moss by 1905 had acquired a set of managers earning as much as fifty dollars a week (more than Moss was paying himself). The presence of these men suggests that Moss had the time as well as the means to look beyond his cloth-sponging business to new ventures.

His first major theatrical project was to lead the syndicate behind the Washington Theatre on Amsterdam Avenue between 149th and 150th Streets. Designed by the Scots-American architect Thomas W. Lamb, who would become one of the foremost theater and cinema designers of the golden age of film, it began operation in the summer of 1910.[1] The *New York Times* has called the Washington, which was built at a cost of $100,000, "the first real 'movie palace' in the city."

As entertainment investments go, the Washington was not high risk. One of the attractions of investing in theaters was that it also meant investing in real estate, a traditional economic advancement strategy for immigrants, one that could provide the basis for mortgage financing in lean years. Describing Marcus Loew, a former penny-arcade owner who went on to create Metro-Goldwyn-Mayer, Douglas Gomery wrote in his 1992 book *Shared Pleasures: A History of Movie Presentation in the United States* that "he ran the operation as a real estate business in which the show could fail but the land was still his." The single biggest coup in the history of the Moss-family business would come in the form of a real estate transaction.

The Washington was followed on January 23, 1913 by Moss & Brill's Hamilton Theatre, a magnificent venue in Hamilton Heights (West Harlem) that hosted both vaudeville and cinema. Also designed by Lamb, it was done up in Renaissance Revival style, and took only six months to build, start to finish. On opening night, there were performances by the house orchestra, an acrobat, several comedians and actors, and short motion pictures. The first theater to bear the Moss name, the Moss & Brill's Hamilton Theatre, was rechristened the B.S. Moss's Hamilton Theatre after partner Solomon Brill sold his share.

As with the Coliseum in Washington Heights, the Hamilton profited immensely from the increased development and foot traffic spurred by the newly constructed Interborough Rapid Transit subway, now known as the 1 Train. It ran from the southern tip of Manhattan to the Bronx and made suburbs such as Hamilton Heights more accessible. New York City, at that moment, was experiencing what the *Real Estate Record and Guide* called "one of the greatest theater building booms in its history." Although Times

---

1   The Washington Theater still stands in Harlem. It has the distinction of being the oldest sur-
     viving theater designed by Lamb, although it has not shown movies since the 1950s. It now
     houses the New Covenant Temple.

Square, with Edward's legendary Palace Theatre at Seventh Avenue and Forty-Seventh Street (it opened two months after the Hamilton), was shaping up as the entertainment capital of Manhattan, many other important theaters were built along the "subway circuit" following the development of public transit. It was a pattern mirrored in major cities across the United States, including Chicago, where the Balaban and Katz Theatre Corporation built its first three cash-cow movie palaces—the Central Park, the Tivoli and the Riviera—in outlying business areas along the trolley networks.

The Hamilton made an impression in New York. After its opening, B.S. Moss began to attract regular notice in the local entertainment press as a film and vaudeville showman. The Moss "brand," even at this early stage, and thanks to Lamb's attractive designs, was trending to the higher end of the market. Like so many other operators, however, he needed quality content.

It was the Lyceum in 1912 that broke the low-brow content cycle. Zukor, who would later found Paramount Pictures, had gone to Europe in search of upscale features to show a U.S. audience. In Paris, he found a four-reel French film (silent, of course; "talkies" would not be exhibited until the 1920s) called *Les amours de la reine* Élisabeth (*The Loves of Queen Elizabeth*). It chronicled a sixteenth-century affair between Elizabeth I and the Earl of Essex. Its star was the famous stage actress Sarah Bernhardt. She played Elizabeth opposite her real-life lover, the Dutch-born Lou Tellegen.

Renamed *Queen Elizabeth* for Americans, the film oozed mainstream respectability and attracted positive reviews when it premiered on July 12, 1912. While Zukor could have saved money by holding the premiere at one of his own facilities, he opted instead for the Lyceum, a lavish Beaux-Arts playhouse, knowing that in the long run the high-rent optics would pay dividends for his brand. The whole endeavor, Zukor later said, went "a long way toward breaking down the prejudice of theatrical people toward the screen."

Although the vaudeville circuits would last through the 1920s, the way was now paved for impressive purpose-built movie houses with proper lighting and sound that would exhibit first-rate popular entertainment to general audiences. Viewers could comfortably immerse themselves in a make-believe world for hours at a time. Exhibitors saw a new kind of customer sitting in their comfortable chairs: well-heeled families, women looking for something to do in their free time, and university students, too. All of these people had money that the nickelodeon owners had been leaving on the table. B.S. Moss would become expert at picking it up.

CHAPTER TWO

A More Beautiful and Sumptuous Edifice

B Y 1919, THE GREAT WAR had been fought and won. Communists had taken control of (most of) Russia. Henry Ford had invented the modern assembly line. The Spanish Flu epidemic had swept the planet. A film called *The Tramp* had turned a formerly obscure London urchin into one of the industry's first millionaire actors. And the World Series that year would be fixed. Through it all, B.S. Moss, by now an established showman in his early forties, never forgot the one fundamental lesson that New York film exhibitors had learned that night at the Lyceum: for their industry to break through to America's middle classes, it had to be respectable in both content and venue. Class was what America wanted, and class was what B.S. Moss gave them, right down to the manners and style he projected in person at gala events, where he appeared in formal attire and played the role of cultural grandee.

Respectability was also Moss's preferred talking point. In the summer of 1919, members of the Vaudeville Managers Protective Association of New York City assembled at the Plaza Hotel to take stock of an industry in the throes of transition. Vaudeville was a mature business, and many of the men in the room already were already converting their properties to movie houses. Nevertheless, Moss, as the evening's toastmaster, painted an upbeat picture of a live entertainment form that, while diminishing in scale, had finally attained the air of respectability and refinement he wanted for it.

In the nineteenth century, he said, one might walk into a down-market Manhattan theater and see "young women who appeared garbed in a more or less imitation of the full dress of dear old Mother Eve after the fall." Scarcely more edifying were the comedy acts of that bygone era, he added, which consisted "of a juggler swallowing yards of tape or a clown wearing a little hat the size of a pillbox."

But "all these things are changed," he said. By hewing to higher quality standards, the men in the room had lifted vaudeville "out of the mire and brought it up to the high standard it now possesses," each of them "vying with one another as to who could put up [the] more beautiful and sumptuous edifice."

At the time he addressed his fellow vaudeville managers, Moss had been in the entertainment business for scarcely a decade; yet already he was a man with a glittering theater empire that was taking shape and stretching from the Bowery all the way up to Washington Heights. He owned eight theaters, including the Broadway, at Broadway and Forty-first Street, his first foray into Manhattan's theater district. That gave him direct control of 19,600 seats, and he had booking arrangements with sixteen other houses. This remarkable growth brought him profit and eminence. Security was another matter.

In 1920, the Shuberts were rumored to be considering an expansion beyond theater to vaudeville. This promised a competitive threat to Moss, but it posed an even bigger threat to Edward Franklin "E. F." Albee, the largest vaudeville impresario in New York. If the well-funded Shuberts were to acquire Moss's chain, it would give them a strong foothold from which to compete with Albee for top talent and films. Moss and Albee solved their mutual problem by rolling their properties into a partnership. Albee purchased a 50% share in Moss's circuit for an undisclosed sum, and The Greater New York Vaudeville Theatres Corporation was born.

The Greater New York circuit controlled 50,000 seats in two dozen venues, sufficient to offer vaudeville entertainers consecutive days of work in New York City for almost a full season, rotating from house to house. The partnership was solid. Moss's name stayed on some of his theaters, and he would always speak glowingly of E. F. Albee, as both model and mentor.

His new partnership did not stop Moss from building new theaters. The B.S. Moss Coliseum opened late in 1920 at Broadway and 181st Street in Washington Heights. The neighborhood was still dotted with undeveloped woodlands that soon would be chopped down to make way for new Irish immigrants. It was by no means a wealthy area, but B.S. Moss was intent on giving it a landmark. He commissioned famed architect Eugene De Rosa to produce an imposing neo-classical design, into which he installed an 85-foot grand lobby, a pipe organ, and more than 3,400 seats. Local historian Jeremy McGraw wrote of the opening night festivities:

Imagine the impression this enormous brand new theater must have given, the third largest in the city (second only to the Hippodrome and the Capitol), its lobby and corridors festooned with flowers from well-wishers: vaudevillians, movie stars, as well as the grateful neighborhood community itself, all milling around, smiling mouths agape in awe at the splendor. The interior was ornately decorated in gray, ivory, French gold, and American Beauty Rose red. Even the bathrooms were richly furnished and included statuary and paintings on the walls . . . Up in the boxes were the big names in Vaudeville, including moguls E. F. Albee and Martin Beck. With its built-in organ, the theater was the ultimate entertainment center. As an overture, music surged from the 25-piece orchestra pit with Ponchielli's magical *Dance of the Hours,* followed by the latest newsreel. Thus warmed up, the audience was then treated to the latest Vaudeville skits from Eddie Foy and his Family, who broke in the new stage and made it shine. The lights were then dimmed to screen the latest silent films, the Harold Lloyd comedy *Get Out and Get Under,* followed by the Norma Talmadge drama *The Branded Woman.* The intermission consisted of selections from Sigmund Romberg's latest musical, *The Magic Melody.* An exit march concluded the show well after midnight.

A year later, Moss would push a step further his idea of "beautiful and sumptuous" theaters and his ambitions for the content they would exhibit. He created the B.S. Moss Cameo Theatre (later known as the Bryant) on West Forty-Second Street near Times Square. It was a purpose-built haven for serious European film.

By the 1920s, purpose-build movie theaters were becoming their own art form. They stood at the vanguard of architectural design. Every element was scrutinized closely by reporters, who published photos of the building interiors, right down to the bathrooms. "Through glazed doors we enter the lobby where the cold tones of the vestibule have been changed for slightly warmer ones," reads a typical review of the Cameo. "The marble base here is of Rosato with pilasters and panels of Sienna marble in which a creamy color predominates and above this is the cornice and a vaulted ceiling." The reviewer concludes that "the Cameo is to theaters what the Petit Trianon [Marie-Antoinette's estate, built in the 1760s by Louis XV] is to royal palaces, an exquisite structure so superbly original in the artistry of its design that it may well stand for years as the finest example of aristocracy in the theater."

Almost all the men who built up the American film exhibition industry in the early part of the twentieth century were, like Moss, creatures of the historical class consciousness of old Europe. One expression of it was the architecture of Moss's new theater, which despite its owner's patriotic inclinations promoted European rather than American aesthetics. Another expression of old-Europe mindset, as Heywood Gould noted, appeared on the screen. Hollywood's ideals of beauty and grace were imported from across the Atlantic: "The fantasies of mud-caked ghettos and dismal tenements were transformed into the American Dream with the rise of stout, sultry, middle-European vamps such as Theda Bara and Vilma Banky. [And] slippery gigolo types like Valentino and Navarro came more from the European ideal of suave, manipulative masculinity than from anything American."

They may have been imported, but the aesthetics of the Cameo and Moss's other theaters resonated with the publics for whom they were built. One public was the press. Another was civic leaders, some of whom still remained skeptical about the cultural influence of movies on public morals.

The most important public was the patrons, many of whom were immigrants familiar with the old-Europe aesthetics, and all of them were capable of recognizing grandeur when they saw it: if they hadn't experienced it in person, they were becoming accustomed to seeing it in film.

In keeping with the lavish surroundings was the superior grade of service enjoyed by patrons at the movie palaces. Gomery in *Shared Pleasures* describes the impressive corps of ushers on attendance to greet arriving customers at every show, most of them college-age teenagers or young adults dressed in red uniforms with white gloves and yellow epaulets: "The ushers responded to patrons with 'yes sir,' or 'no ma'am' and all requests had to end with a 'thank you.'" Even rowdy customers who were escorted out of the theater were led away "with propriety and sensitivity to emphasize that if they opted to be well-behaved that they were welcome to return."

Extravagant as they were, Moss's theaters were designed with the bottom line in mind. The grander the experience, the higher the ticket prices. In addition to beautiful fixtures designed by the likes of Lamb and Irving T. Bush (who designed the Bush Terminal Building, now more commonly referred to as Bush Tower, to which the Cameo adjoined), Moss's audiences were treated the latest advances in air circulation, crowd control, and commercial efficiency. Most theaters now featured air-conditioning, an innovation that would lead to massive sales increases in the summer months, when some viewers would go to the movies to escape the heat, regardless of what was on the marquee.

Still other features of Moss's theaters were invisible to the patron's eye but important to his or her security. The same periodicals that gushed over Moss's cornices and marble panels noted the modern projectionists' room, including "a Safe-T-First enclosed film cabinet." Nitrocellulose film was fantastically flammable, and would continue burning even when fully submerged in water. Movie-house fires caused by the burning of nitrocellulose film produced some horrific tragedies, including a 1929 fire at the Glen Cinema in Paisley, Scotland, that claimed the lives of sixty-nine children. Hence the attraction of the Safe-T-First cabinet.

* * *

Although B.S. Moss was now accepted around New York as an accomplished showman, his everyday life was perhaps more intense than that of any modern movie executive. He found himself with more than a dozen theaters to stock with daily entertainment. Each hybrid show might involve hundreds of moving parts, from live dancers, jugglers, tumblers and musicians, to the technicians required to operate the still finicky and unreliable technology used to project films. Content turned over rapidly, and critics could be scathing, taking pains to point out if a pretty actress looked overweight or a comedian seemed hung over.

Since many homes, businesses and hotels didn't have telephones, merely getting hold of an actor or projectionist to fill an open date might take days. In one episode that made its way to a New York City entertainment columnist, a famous comedian touring the Midwest found out that he'd be starring in a B.S. Moss vaudeville show only after he saw his face staring back at him from an advertisement contained in a local newspaper.

Then, as now, the viewing public was ruthless about what it liked and didn't like, requiring Moss to adjust constantly to evolving tastes and trends. If he didn't adjust, he'd be pushed out by others who did. Another complicating factor in Moss's decisions was the fragmented nature of the entertainment marketplace. The mass market was still in its infancy. Moss had to monitor and accommodate the particular tastes of each neighborhood in which he exhibited. What slayed the Irish might fall flat with the Germans. His publicity scrapbooks, some of them surviving in Moss archives to this day, contain clippings in a dozen different melting-pot languages.

A dearth of quality films continued to present yet another problem. The industry was taking its time about graduating from shorter novelty reels. Until the early 1920s, few Hollywood producers were making feature-length dramas. When they did finally produce them in volume, another problem arose: the industry organized into vertically integrated anti-competitive trusts, which played their own movies at their own theaters so as to freeze out "independents" like B.S. Moss. It was a fundamentally anti-competitive arrangement that eventually would lead to a landmark 1948 Supreme Court judgment, United States v. Paramount Pictures, Inc., which had the effect of busting up Hollywood's exploitative old-time studio system permanently. It was a landmark in the history of antitrust law, but it took decades for the industry to comply fully with the judgment. And so, Moss and his successors were required to navigate the industry's vertically integrated, oligopolistic structure until well into the modern blockbuster era. The principal way of doing so was having enough seats in a circuit that the producers couldn't ignore it.

Having early developed a personal interest in film as a medium for art and education, B.S. Moss found the lack of quality reels intolerable and, for a time, he took matters into his own hands. Between 1916 and 1920, the B.S. Moss Motion Picture Corporation produced silent films, one of which, a 50-minute melodrama called *The Salamander* (1916), survives in watchable print form at the Library of Congress in Washington, D.C.

The Salamander was a departure from many films of this early era, cautionary tales about female ingénues whose lives are wrecked when they abandon the familiar rituals and values of home life. In 1917, for instance, B.S. Moss' circuit advertised a seven-week cycle of five-act "photoplays" (theatrical performances filmed for cinematic distribution) called *Seven Deadly Sins*, with each instalment dedicated to a different vice. The plot, prospective viewers were informed, centered around Eve Leslie, who is "young, beautiful, appealing. Wealth, luxury [and] social success are within her reach. But they have a price. The men and women who have the power to give Eve her heart's desires are pawns of Seven Deadly Sins. They will give her what she wants, but her soul will be stained in the getting."

Offering a bold feminist twist on these trite, moralizing tales, *The Salamander* proved to be a critically acclaimed blockbuster. Its country-girl heroine, Dore Baxter (played by Ruth Findlay), leaves home to track down the evil con man who cast her family into poverty, and then marries the handsome millionaire who helps her get the job done. The work on which the film was based, Owen Johnson's 1914 book of the same name, was the first novel of any note to set a flapper as its protagonist. On the cover of the first edition, Baxter is described as "a girl of the present day in revolt—adventurous, eager, and unafraid" who "comes roving from somewhere out of the immense reaches of the nation, revolting against the commonplace of an inherited narrowness."

The American film industry always has reflected the wider political and social attitudes of society at large. Sadly, this includes the openly expressed bigotries of the early and mid-twentieth century. (As we shall see later, it wasn't until the 1960s that film producers and exhibitors began to seriously grapple with the racist representations embedded in their medium.) But the available evidence suggests that B.S Moss did tend toward views that were liberal by the standards of his time, at least in regard to first-wave feminism (as we would now call it).

One of Moss's most famous collaborators was Margaret Sanger (1879–1966), a brave activist who opened America's first birth-control clinic (she was the person who first popularized the very term "birth control") and sowed the organizational seeds that eventually became Planned Parenthood. When a sympathetic documentary was released about Sanger in April 1917—simply titled *Birth Control*—Moss's company was listed as producer.

In the promotional materials leading up to the release, *Birth Control* was described as "five reels of stirring, varied and picturesque exposition of the vital and dramatic phases of the crusade that sent its martyr [Sanger] to a prison cell [for running an illegal birth control clinic in Brooklyn], from which she has just been freed." There is also an accompanying "certificate of genuineness" from Sanger, presumably meant to assure exhibitors that no other competing film of this type would be produced. It read: "This is the only picture on Birth Control in which I shall appear. Part of the profits go to extending our cause."

Unfortunately, the public never saw the movie which was banned by license commissioner George Bell before its first public screening at New York's Park Theatre on the grounds that the subject matter was "immoral, indecent, and contrary to public welfare." The film was screened once before several hundred reporters and activists and never shown again. There are, to my knowledge, no known surviving copies. All we have left are accounts such as those provided by New York State Supreme Court judge Nathan Bijur, who described the plot of the movie in a court opinion (temporarily, alas) setting aside the license commissioner's decision:

The scenario of the play may be briefly summarized as follows: It presents a number of pictures showing the poverty and misery frequently associated with the presence of large families of children among the poor. It illustrates the sufferings of one or more women to whom childbirth means serious danger to life. It then presents pictures of comfort among the rich where smaller families are supposed to obtain. Intermingled with these are pictures of Mrs. Sanger acting as a nurse. She is strongly tempted to advise some of the suffering poor women on the subject of birth control, but refrains from giving such information because it is forbidden by law. [New York State] Penal Law, § 1142. Finally, she concludes to defy the law and opens a clinic to disseminate information on this subject. There is then portrayed a movement undertaken by persons of means who engage detectives to suppress her efforts. The clinic established by Mrs. Sanger is exhibited crowded by poor women . . . It may perhaps be inferred from the pictures that the rich violate the law by employing contraceptive methods of which the poor are ignorant.

The legal fight over *Birth Control* became part of the generation-long fight over censorship of the film industry; a fight that didn't fully end until the 1960s. But that fight would be left to others, as Moss would leave the film-production business shortly after the end of World War I, and focus on the art of exhibition, a decision whose repercussions will be analyzed in more detail in the next chapter.

Moss would continue to break new ground through the Roaring Twenties. In 1928, he played host at his Colony Theatre when a cartoon scamp named Mickey Mouse first hit the big screen with *Steamboat Willie*. The cartoon marked the start of a lengthy business relationship, with many other Disney classics going on to openings at Moss theaters. To this day, the boardroom of the Moss offices in New York display telegrams sent to Charles Moss from Walt Disney himself.

* * *

Having sought and achieved both success and respectability, B.S. Moss, to use the old cliché, was a "model immigrant," and in historical terms he existed at a turning point in the history of North American Jewry.

Until the late nineteenth century, there had long been a relatively small, generally well-assimilated Jewish population in urban centers such as New York and Boston, making up a baseline community of about 300,000 in total. But these well-established Jews were completely dwarfed in number by the poor arrivals who showed up *en masse* during the last two decades of the twentieth century, men and women fleeing the anti-Jewish pogroms that tore through Russia, Belarus, Lithuania, Moldova, Ukraine, Latvia and Poland. The Warsaw pogrom, which took place just months after B.S. Moss and his family set sail for America in 1880, had played out in typical fashion: a fire scare at a crowded church had given rise to a deadly stampede which some claimed had been the deliberate work of pickpockets looking to prey on a panicky crowd. When a baseless rumor spread that a pair of Jewish criminals had been spotted at the church, a mob attacked Jewish homes and businesses, and days of violence followed.

To the small, largely wealthy population of established American Jews, many of whose ancestors had come over from Germany generations earlier, these freshly arrived co-religionists could seem like migrants from another planet: tailors, peasants and laborers who grew up in ghettos or impoverished farming communities, often beaten down psychologically and physically within the semi-feudal societies of eastern Europe. As Hadassa Kosak wrote in *Cultures of Opposition: Jewish Immigrant Workers, New York City, 1881-1905*, many German Jews "regarded the East European immigrants as clannish, incorrigibly dirty in their everyday habits, overly inclined towards peddling, at best a source of social embarrassment, at worst a cause of anti-Semitism." For their part, the new arrivals tended to reject the top-down bureaucratic oversight of established Jewish organizations in favor of the more informal, kin-based, *landsmanshaft* mutual-aid societies that grew out of their villages in the old country.

There was also a concern, foreshadowing more modern anxieties about Muslims, that the new arrivals would exhibit, in the words of one activist from the period, an excessively "rigid adherence to the rites of Judaism."

A sort of de facto segregation sprouted up within North American Jewry, with synagogues and civic institutions being dominated by either the old guard or the new arrivals. In most communities, this intra-Jewish cultural gulf wouldn't be fully bridged until well into the twentieth century.

The divide between the two groups was not as simple as rich uncle versus poor cousin. Despite the massive gulf in wealth and refinement, the new arrivals brought with them a feisty capitalist spirit, a resource that tends to mark all waves of immigrants whose faculties are unleashed in lands of opportunity where they suddenly are unburdened by old-world tethers of faith, race and caste. More generally, these Jews also brought with them a profound sense of the epic possibilities that the *idea* of the United States represented. Native-born Americans of the Gilded Age had witnessed numerous financial busts and panics, epic political scandals and the murder of two presidents within sixteen years, not to mention the Civil War, which had taken 620,000 lives (one in fifty Americans). Their America wasn't the paradise that Hollywood's largely foreign-born architects would encode in film.

B.S. Moss bridged these two Jewish worlds as a sort of perfect hybrid. On one hand, the historical record suggests that he spoke, dressed and wrote as a well-mannered gentleman of the era, essential qualities for a business manager seeking to lease and buy respectable theaters, raise capital and lure top talent into unproven new fields. On the other hand, he channeled the ambition, imagination, and patriotism of a man with humble roots, whose relationship with America remained in its honeymoon phase. This compound skill—to "walk with Kings" without losing "the common touch," as Kipling put it—seems to have defined B.S. Moss's personality. His entry in a century-old who's-who volume called *Distinguished Jews of America* informs us that "Mr. Moss makes no pretenses . . . No frocks or frills about him; no affected airs . . . He looks down upon no one and treats everyone as his equal . . . a keen, intelligent and sober-minded man."

CHAPTER THREE

Women Discover
the Movies

THAT QUALITY, FULL-LENGTH motion pictures were slow to fill America's cinemas does not mean there were no hits. Then, as now, the measure of success was gross receipts: how many people paid money to see a particular firm. From 1911 to 1920, the top-grossing U.S. film was *The Birth of a Nation*, a Civil War epic that earned a domestic box-office haul of about $10 million. That massive haul set a new economic benchmark, and it would be a decade before another film broke the $10-million mark: King Vidor's *The Big Parade* (followed a few months later by the even more popular *Ben-Hur²*). Throughout the entire period from 1911 to 1930, fewer than forty films were true hits that broke the $1-million mark.

---

2   The term "blockbuster" didn't exist until World War II, when it was coined to describe a massive aerial bomb that could be used to destroy whole city blocks, and the first movies that were described as "block busters" (the term was then often written out as two separate words) were war movies such as *Bombardier* (1943) and the acclaimed documentary *With the Marines at Tarawa* (1944).

And so, in B.S. Moss's time, as in the modern era, decisions about what films to show had enormous financial implications for an exhibitor, especially since each theater had only one screen, meaning an owner couldn't cover his bets, multiplex-style. The decisions were streamlined somewhat because the volume of available films was not high, and because some of the best films would have been off-limits to Moss and other independent exhibitors, thanks to the vertically integrated studio system that prevailed until after World War II. But where content decisions were required, exhibitors of Moss's generation had very little information to work with, and sometimes found themselves buying movies based on little more than title, marketing materials, and the names (or pseudonyms) of the film's main stars. In our own era, by comparison, choices tend to be simpler: if you go down the list of top twenty-five domestic grossing films for the period from 2010 to 2019, you'll find that every one of them featured established Hollywood stars with their own built-in fan bases, and all but five were reboots, remakes, sequels, or adaptations of tried and tested franchises.

Like Moss's *The Salamander*, many of the earliest hit movies were based on novels or plays, but these underlying sources often provided a scant basis for predicting the success of a film adaptation. The aforementioned 1915 blockbuster, *Birth of a Nation,* was based on a virulently racist and widely denounced book called *The Clansman: A Historical Romance of the Ku Klux Klan.* It was also three hours long, much longer than normal fare for the period. No one could have predicted that it was going to become a once-in-a-generation hit.

The absence of a reliable stream of quality, full-length feature films meant unending financial pressures on theater operators. Revenues would boom and bust but costs were constant and high. Moss had overhead. Even before his shows opened, he was paying property taxes, insurance, utilities and wages for accountants and office staff. To exhibit a movie required a small army of ushers, servers, and ticket takers, as well as musical accompaniment for what were then silent films. In small-town theaters, musical accompaniment was usually nothing more than a piano. A 1921 news item about Moss's construction of a 3,500-seat "photoplay-vaudeville" theater at the corner of 161st Street and Prospect Avenue in the Bronx described the movie screen as towering over "a symphony orchestra of 40 pieces, a

mammoth pipe organ," and facilities for "operati'
pipe organs used in silent film not only accompa
vided such useful sound effects as gunshots, dooru.
And because no feature film was yet viewed as standa.
vaudeville, in one form or another, was kept alive in theaters,
costs of running them. Moss continued to be one of the largest .
ers of musical, theatrical, and comic talent in New York. Working behi.
the talent was another army of stagehands and technicians, directors and
conductors, booking agents, and even animal wranglers.

Not only was running a movie theater with a daily variety show an
expensive proposition, but as crowds became more sophisticated, the
aesthetics required were more exacting, too. As the Twenties progressed, theaters began to organize their entertainment spectacles around their feature
film attractions. When Moss opened his opulent Colony Theatre at 53rd
Street and Broadway on Christmas Day, 1924 with *The Thief of Baghdad*,
the symphonic accompaniment was led by none other than Edwin Franko
Goldman, still known today as one of the period's greatest band composers
of his era. Before the movie began, Goldman entertained the crowd with
his orchestra's rendition of the Second Hungarian Rhapsody, followed by a
new title dedicated to the theater itself, the "Colony March." There was still
more: an operatic mezzo-soprano singing a selection from "Ave Maria," and
"a prologue tableau, staged by Alexander Oumansky, offer[ing] a colorful
introduction to the feature picture."

Competition among the many theaters in the New York area, and the
ability of patrons to move with ease via public transport to whichever venue
had the most enticing show, meant that B.S. Moss also had to spend money
on advertising. He was not reluctant to do so, but he was disinclined to
put himself forward in the advertisements as some impresarios did. Then,
as now, there were movies that reflected the rough-and-tumble cultural
influences of vaudeville, and others that reflected the more refined aesthetics appropriate to a movie palace. Moss presented saw himself as a popular
showman and a high-minded cultural grandee. When he spoke to the
media, his tone was carefully cultivated to come across as a reluctant mogul
whose main objective was to bring the finest and most edifying forms of

rtainment to New York City's masses. When the carnival barker's role ᵼs required, he assigned it to an underling.

In 1925, for instance, the Colony had a hit on its hands with *The Homemaker*, a farce about a husband who stays home while his wife goes out to work. Moss put out a two-page spread splashed liberally with rave reviews from the theater's manager, one Howard McCoy, complete with the bespectacled fellow's picture. As with the Moss family's Criterion property in Times Square many decades later, the Colony was a marquee theater where a film taking its star turn wouldn't just drum up interest among ordinary filmgoers, but also other theater operators, to whom Moss would sub-license exhibition rights. "'Get the women and you ensure big business' is the oldest axiom of the show business," proclaimed McCoy. "*The Homemaker* has every essential to hit with the ladies. Bet your shirt on it to get over big. WE DID AND IT DID."

Moss's files contain mountains of clever ad campaigns, many of them quoting film reviews in all the many languages of polyglot Manhattan. There were no end of movie reviewers, even in the early days of the art. As one would expect, their responses to individual films range from over-the-moon positive (and thus likely to be included in an advertising campaign) to scathing. Of the Colony-screened drama *Hell's Highroad*, critic Regina Cannon said that the film's poor quality demonstrated that thirty-two-year-old star Leatrice Joy (aka Leatrice Johanna Zeidler) was clearly over the hill: "Her clothes are a fright, her attempts at emoting ludicrous, and her general appearance un-Leatrice-like in the extreme."

There were other sources quoted in film advertisements, too, these of a type that would seem more mysterious to modern filmgoers. The ad for *The Homemaker*, for instance, cited something called the Pasadena, CA "Board of Review" to the effect that viewing the film had been "an occasion of great delight for our [members]."

Like exhibitors in every era, B.S. Moss always had to contend with the possibility that a film in one of his theaters might bomb, but as we saw with the 1917 documentary *Birth Control*, theater owners also had to contend with the possibility that they might buy or license a film that couldn't be shown because the movie was rejected by local review boards.

In the 1915 decision *Mutual Film Corporation v. Industrial Commission of Ohio*, the U.S. Supreme Court determined that movies were a species of commerce, not art, and so could be regulated outside the protections afforded by the First Amendment. It wasn't until 1952 that the ruling would be overturned in a case called *Joseph Burstyn, Inc. v. Wilson*. In the intervening decades, producers and exhibitors were governed by often overlapping rules that restricted exhibition to (in the words of the Ohio statute at issue in *Mutual Film Corporation*) "only such films as are in the judgment and discretion of the board of censors of a moral, educational or amusing and harmless character." In many cases, violations could be punished with jail time. Adding insult to injury, film companies often had to pay the review boards for the privilege of having their works evaluated.

While such policies will strike modern readers as instruments of bald-faced censorship, the text of the *Mutual Film Corporation* case helps contextualize the prevailing attitude among public officials, steeped as they were in the idea of film as a sort of carnival amusement. "[Movies] may be mediums of thought, but so are many things," wrote Justice Joseph McKenna in his opinion. "So is the theater, the circus, and all other shows and spectacles." By the court's logic, in other words, the regulation of film content wasn't entirely different from, say, a health-and-safety law governing what kind of live animal acts could be performed at a vaudeville show.

At the same time, the judgment betrays the popular fear that film, then becoming America's dominant entertainment medium, could be used to propagandize large swathes of the population in unwholesome or even malevolent ways. "Their power of amusement and, it may be, education, the audiences they assemble, not of women alone nor of men alone, but together, not of adults only, but of children, make them the more insidious in corruption by a pretense of worthy purpose or if they should degenerate from worthy purpose," wrote Justice McKenna. "They take their attraction from the general interest, eager and wholesome it may be, in their subjects, but a prurient interest may be excited and appealed to. Besides, there are some things which should not have pictorial representation in public places and to all audiences."

Even among civic groups, there was surprisingly high support for film censorship. This was the era of Prohibition, and many of the same liberal activists (as we would now call them) who supported women's suffrage also were teetotalers who campaigned against alcohol and public immorality more generally. This included public nudity and the sort of lowbrow burlesque theatrical tradition in which the nickelodeon trade was rooted. American Catholics became especially influential in the effort to suppress controversial films and, in 1933, even formed an organization called the National Legion of Decency, which rated films on a scale of A, B or C (with C standing for "condemned"). There was also a quasi-public body called the New York Society for the Suppression of Vice, whose members could earn half of the value of fines levied when they discovered newspapers, books or plays with smutty themes.

Films themselves partook in this crusade for decency. With millions of rural Americans migrating to large cities every year, and many of them falling victim to the vices of city life, real and imagined, themes of temptation and ruin were huge box-office draws. An appreciative *Morning Telegraph* review of the 1924 film *Broken Laws* describes it as "the story of an over-indulgent mother who spoils her young son. He grows to young manhood and is caught in the mad whirl of jazz parties and roadhouse carousings." The reviewer notes that "so enthusiastically has [the film] been received by the women's clubs and civic welfare organizations throughout the United States . . . that arrangements have been made for a Broadway showing of the picture [at] B.S. Moss's Cameo Theatre." For anyone in the entertainment business, in other words, keeping the daily fare on the moral straight and narrow wasn't just the law: it was good business."

* * *

Outside the conference room at the Bow Tie Partners offices, there is a framed letter, dated September 5, 1944, addressed to one "Master Charles B. Moss, Jr." of 130 East 75th Street, otherwise known as B.S. Moss's grandson Charley. It reads:

My dear Charles:

When you are old enough to read this letter, you will learn that I welcomed you to this great city of New York on your arrival, as one of its citizens-to-be, and I wished you many years of happiness and good health and contentment. In order to give you tangible evidence of that welcome, and of my great regard for you and your parents, I enclose a War Bond for $25.00, made out to your order and hope to go with you to the bank when it becomes due. At this time, a great world-wide war is at its height, and please God we all hope it will end soon and no further wars during your lifetime.

The letter is signed by B.S. Moss's brother Paul, the grand-uncle of the then newly born "Master Charles," who had come in to the world eight days earlier. Off in the top left corner of the framed version appear the words "Office of the Commissioner." And though New York City has had many commissioners of one type of another, everyone who mattered at the time would have known the precise nature of this man's remit. At the height of his powers, in fact, Paul Moss, New York City Commissioner of Licenses, was arguably more famous, and certainly more powerful, than his older brother Benjamin.

As a youth, Paul had performed on stage as a blackface comic. (One source identifies him as having performed in a duo called Clark and Williams, which apparently was known for a tune called "We Are Two Dandy Coachmen.") When Paul got older, he helped Benjamin produce movies and operate theaters. He also produced the 1931 thriller *Subway Express*, and a play called *The Mongrel* starring Rudolph Schildkraut, a legendary Hapsburg-era Austrian stage actor who would become famous in America for his role as the High Priest Caiaphas in Cecil B. DeMille's 1927 film, *The King of Kings*.

All of these achievements, however, would appear as mere footnotes to Paul Moss's principal claim to fame as gutter-cleaner for Fiorello H. La Guardia, New York City's mayor between 1934 and 1945. As *Time* magazine indelicately put it in 1937, "Paul Moss is a big, grey-haired Jew whom

Mayor La Guardia picked to be New York's Commissioner of Licenses when he turned Tammany out of City Hall three years ago. Since the power to license is the power to reform, Commissioner Moss, who is as notable for his integrity as for his dapper dress, lost no time suppressing short-weight ice dealers, market racketeers [and] dirty magazine publishers."

A conspiracy theorist would be forgiven for noting that Paul and Benjamin's interests were aligned when it came to keeping the city's well-known entertainment areas respectable. During the early years of the Great Depression, burlesque shows began migrated to Times Square, occupying facilities that had been abandoned by legitimate theater companies that had run out of cash. The bawdier fare presented women in a state of quasi-striptease and promoted a type of comedian (the so-called "nance") who presented himself as a barely closeted homosexual. These acts were crowd pleasers, but also legally risky in a city bound by the Wales Padlock Law, which prohibited "depicting or dealing with, the subject of sex degeneracy, or sex perversion," including homosexuality in virtually any context. Consistent with the appalling homophobia that marked the era, even Radclyffe Hall's lesbian novel *The Well of Loneliness* was banned at one point, on the theory, as one city magistrate put it, that "the weaker members of society" must be protected from "corrupt, depraving and lecherous influences."

New York City had no shortage of morality monitors during this era, but Moss's tenure as Licensing Commissioner took puritanism into a new phase, and with fresh allies. The influx of burlesque into Times Square catalyzed the creation of an entity called the 42nd Street Property Owners Association, or POA. As Andrea Friedman wrote in a 1996 study of the campaign against New York burlesque houses, "members of the POA witnessed firsthand the Depression's effect on Times Square merchants, watching as storefronts increasingly became occupied by proprietors who catered to working-class and lower-middle-class customers. Many of the organization's members blamed the new burlesque theaters for this state of affairs, claiming that their presence chased away more respectable merchants, drove down property values, and generally 'cheapened' the street."

The POA's agenda dovetailed with that of La Guardia, who loved populist stunts such as burning obscene books and magazines, and taking a sledgehammer to illegal slot machines. La Guardia also seized on lurid sex crimes, such as the 1936 rape and murder of a young writer named Nancy Evans Titterton, to demonize burlesques and similar entertainments as mind-addling engines of violence and perversion. Under political cover of public hysteria, Paul Moss was able to close down New York's last three burlesque theaters in 1942.

Almost eight decades later, Paul Moss's name is still sometimes used as a byword for social panic and repressive sexual attitudes. The 2013 Broadway show *The Nance* included Moss as an unseen character in the crowd, a foil for "Chauncey," the gay stage entertainer played by Nathan Lane, whose turmoil drives a plot that plays out amidst the 1930s-era crackdowns of the La Guardia administration. At one point, Chauncey described Moss as a "confirmed bachelor," suggesting that Moss is not only cruel and intolerant, but a closeted hypocrite besides.

It is true that Paul Moss was indeed a lifelong bachelor (whether gay or not), and that he pushed through some of the most notorious policies of the La Guardia administration. But *The Nance* presents only one side of the man. Much like the suffragettes and teetotalers of the early twentieth century who also embraced racism and even crackpot eugenics, Paul Moss had a decidedly mixed legacy as a social reformer.

As his *New York Times* obituary noted, many of the new policies Moss brought in were actually liberal and humane. Prior to his tenure, children weren't permitted to attend movies unattended, and would often loiter outside until some stranger agreed to escort them inside (a practice that, in itself, posed all manner of unsettling risks). In 1936, Moss had a law passed that allowed children to enter on their own "provided they sat in a separate section, with a matron in attendance." He shut down genuinely unsavory business operators, such as grifters and pawnshops, which preyed on tourists, minors, and the unwary. He began rigorous implementation of a much-abused law that had been designed to prioritize wounded World War I veterans in the awarding of newsstand licenses. He also pushed through a 1941 law that permitted such newspaper vendors to sell their products from enclosed kiosks, instead of standing around on the sidewalks as Paul's brother Benjamin had done as a boy. As any visitor to New York City knows, those kiosks exist to this day.

There's more. On July 8, 1945, four weeks before the *Enola Gay* dropped an atomic bomb on Hiroshima, a black military veteran named Jacob Johnson was refused entry to two beachside bathhouses in the Rockaway Park area of Queens. Along with other black bathers, Johnson, who'd served as an anti-aircraft gunner in the South Pacific during the war, summoned a police officer to confront the bathhouse owners. According to news reports, the managers responded by simply closing their ticket windows. When Johnson came to Moss with the story, the License Commissioner held hearings, and concluded that the businesses had "willfully and knowingly discriminated against Negro citizens by refusing to grant them admission . . . Such conditions cannot and will not be tolerated." As the newspapers reported, it was the first action of its kind under New York State's then-recently enacted Law Against Discrimination, thus making this scourge of the gay performing arts world and former blackface performer something of a human-rights pioneer, a complicated legacy to be sure.

For the Moss family, Paul Moss delivered a more particular kind of legacy. During the Great Depression, Times Square really was at risk of losing its reputation as a first-rate entertainment hub, as legitimate theaters were replaced, as one critic put it, by "burlesque halls, vaudeville stages, and dime houses." If things had continued to deteriorate, there would have been nothing to discourage the city's highbrow entertainment moguls from migrating completely to other areas, such as the Upper West Side, where Robert Moses' Lincoln Square Renewal Project (now known as Lincoln Center) took shape in the 1950s.

Paul Moss's puritanical campaign, however reviled by many artists, helped maintain Times Square's public respectability, and facilitated the golden age of Broadway theater that began with *Oklahoma!* in 1943 and extended into the 1960s, a period that overlapped with the heyday of the Moss family's flagship Criterion Theatre, which became the site of countless blockbuster premieres during the tenure of B.S. Moss's son Charles and grandson Charley.

In time, Paul Moss's clean-up operation also would provide a template for the analogous transformation of Times Square engineered under Mayor Rudolph Giuliani in the 1990s, after the area had once again fallen into decay, this time at the hands of porn merchants and street hustlers. It was B.S. Moss who created the family's film exhibition business. But it was Uncle Paul who sowed the seeds for its future survival.

CHAPTER FOUR

An Art Form Matures

O NE OF THE MYSTERIES OF B.S. Moss's career, and the entire arc of the Moss family business, is why his film-exhibition circuit remained a relatively contained regional operation at a time when his contemporaries were building larger national chains integrated with Hollywood-based studios, or pulling up stakes and moving to California to build their own studios. Was it a lack of ambition? A lack of resources? Or something else? Whatever the reason, this choice would seem to have something to do with the business's ability to remain family run and to flourish over four generations.

Again, B.S. Moss saw some of his contemporaries do exceedingly well out west. The likes of Adolph Zukor, Jesse L. Lasky, Carl Laemmle, Samuel Goldwyn and Louis B. Mayer built massive companies combining studios and theater chains, controlling the profits generated by their films at all points in the pipeline. They became rich and famous and were celebrated for the contributions to American culture. B.S.'s son, Charles B. Moss, Sr., and grandson, Charley, toured the Warner Bros. lot in 1963 and saw first-hand what their own family fortunes might have looked like if B.S. had followed the lead of the early moguls. Even after the studio system had run afoul of the law, there were still fantastic fortunes to be made in the production of movies. Yet none of the Mosses left the east coast, and none expanded nationally.

The temptations would have been strongest for B.S. because for him the studio system was a viable business model, just waiting to be adopted, and his status as an independent operator competing against the Hollywood oligopolies was always precarious. He had no guaranteed access to quality movies, and the studios made it difficult for him to expand into new markets.

Perhaps the best evidence of B.S. Moss's concern for the might of the studios is that in 1936 he opened the Criterion and brought in a Warner Brothers in-law as a partner. Harry Charnas was the husband of Rose Warner. The hope was that affiliation would help the Criterion get access to first-run Warner Brothers product. It was a nice idea, but it didn't work. The films were not forthcoming, and the partnership was summarily dissolved. Charnas is now remembered by Hollywood primarily for his role in opening a bowling alley on the Warner Brothers lot.

So why did B.S. stay in New York? There were several reasons. Manhattan has always been the money capital of America and, indeed, the world, and B.S. Moss (like his successors) understood that a special kind of security comes from operating in a market where people have disposable income and business owners have ready access to capital. The Mosses have never been wildcatters, as many of the movie pioneers were. B.S. also appreciated the stability that comes with bricks and mortar businesses sitting on valuable real estate. However innovative and creative he may have been in some aspects of his operations he was at bottom a conservative businessman.

The timing of B.S. Moss's immigration to the United States and his experience on arrival provides another reason for staying in Manhattan. He grew up in New York as part of a large, mutually supportive family (albeit one that was impoverished in his early years). The city was welcoming and provided enough opportunity for him to find success relatively swiftly, and by the time he did, he had a strong sense of rooted community identity. By all available accounts, B.S. got on well with his brothers, took care of his ailing father, stayed close to his mother, the family's emotional lynchpin, and became active within New York City's larger Jewish community.

A lot of the early moguls were not as young as B.S. Moss on arriving in America. Universal Studios founder Carl Laemmle immigrated from

Germany when he was already seventeen. Samuel Goldwyn (his name supplying the G in "MGM") fled Poland as a teenager after his father died. Paramount founder Adolph Zukor was a Hungarian orphan who sailed for the United States at the age of eighteen. These were men cut off from their families and the old norms and restraints they'd known as children, especially once they got rich. Of the early Hollywood giants who'd grown up in North America, many emerged from fractured or itinerant households. MGM's Louis B. Mayer was a junk-peddling street urchin from New Brunswick who decamped for Boston, where he spent his days diving for scrap metal in the city's harbor, before renovating a burlesque theater.

These men are lionized for their ambition and up-from-nothing social mobility, but they sacrificed a lot to get where they did. Untempered and unsupported by loving families and stable communities, they chased their ambitions all the way to Hollywood where filmmakers were setting up shop during the early years of the twentieth century primarily as a means to evade the monopoly imposed by Thomas Edison's Motion Picture Patents Company. Hollywood at the time was a snake-infested scrubland punctuated by a few homes, orchards, chicken farms and bean fields. One of the reasons the early titans of Hollywood became so powerful, so quickly, is that there was no incumbent power to displace.

By 1918, there were seventy-five film companies operating in the area, and Hollywood had the air of a gold-rush town. As with all gold-rush towns, it was filled with hard young men desperate to make their fortunes. Given the absence of an established social order or civic culture, these environments tend to become dominated by small groups of alpha males who are free to allow their scarred souls whatever expression they desire. The results in Hollywood were often glamorous, but just as often morally bankrupt. The early moguls turned the town into a ruthless corporate monarchy of celluloid kings and starlet harems where money ruled, talent was ruthlessly exploited, and everyone believed his own press clippings.

Fans of the 2016 Coen brothers film *Hail, Caesar!* will remember Josh Brolin playing the role of real-life Hollywood fixer Eddie Mannix, who's tasked with finding a key studio actor (played by George Clooney) gone missing during the filming of a sword-and-sandals epic. The plot is fictional, but Mannix was a real historical figure who worked for decades at MGM alongside publicity head Howard Strickland, covering up every imaginable kind of celebrity scandal, from affairs and addictions to secret pregnancies, gay sex, and even homicide.

In *The Fixers: Eddie Mannix, Howard Strickling and the MGM Publicity Machine*, his 2005 book about MGM's toxic internal culture of the 1920s, 1930s and 1940s, author E.J. Fleming centered his narrative on the tragically real story of German-born MGM producer Paul Bern (1889-1932), who was found dead in his bedroom with a gunshot wound to his head, just two months after marrying actress and sex symbol Jean Harlow. Witnesses had seen a limousine speeding off the night before, possibly containing Bern's mentally unbalanced common-law wife from the east coast, Dorothy Millette (who took her own life just two days later, by leaping from a steamboat into the Sacramento River). It was a double tragedy, later compounded by Harlow's own early death in 1937.

This scene was rendered yet more surreal and unsettling by the chain of events that unfolded immediately after servants discovered Bern's body. Before police had a chance to respond, the entire brain trust of MGM was whisked to the house. "Standing around Bern's body, already showing signs of advanced rigor mortis, the group was facing a defining moment, a monumental scandal," Fleming wrote. "They all knew who murdered Bern and why. They had always known the truth [about Bern's previous relationship]. And that Harlow knew. They also understood that [if publicized], it would end her career and ruin the studio. They assumed Bern had been murdered by Dorothy Millette. They knew Millette was still his wife."

And so Fleming concluded that, on that morning of September 5, 1932, while they still had control of the evidence, Mannix, Strickling, and their MGM colleagues created the outline of a theory of death that would become the official version: Bern committed suicide because he harbored some secret shame (which a later whisper campaign identified as sexual dysfunction). "The murder was becoming just another movie scenario written for the public," Fleming wrote. The studio even brought over a cameraman to take pictures that supported the suicide theory, and Strickland called his contacts at newspapers before making the call to the police.

This is just one tawdry story of many that emerged from the early days of Hollywood, but it serves to illustrate the vast cultural gulf that then existed between B.S. Moss's New York and Eddie Mannix's Hollywood. Louis B. Mayer and Jack Warner were perfect specimens of early Hollywood. B.S. Moss was not. It is impossible to imagine him being in Paul Bern's home on the morning of September 5, 1932, and collaborating in the ghoulish noir project (as Fleming presents it) of faking a suicide.

Of course, New York City's entertainment industry was hardly a den of boy scouts. And Moss himself had to deal daily with many notorious scoundrels, not least the Shubert brothers, whose dishonest and at times truly loathsome business practices have become etched into Broadway lore.[3] But, as it happens, we know something about Moss's feelings about such men. A set of World War I-era letters that Moss exchanged with Lee Shubert survive in the Shubert Archive, which sits atop the Lyceum Theatre, across Forty-Fifth Street from the Bow Tie offices.

In their twilight years, many of Hollywood's giants would endow charities or put their name on public buildings, often as a means to rehabilitate their public images following careers marred by scandal, broken friendships and cutthroat deal-making. Moss, by contrast, began giving back to the community when he was a young man, already with a strong reputation. In particular, he took on the leadership of the Krakauer Beneficial Society, through which New York's wealthier and established Jews assisted poor families arriving from Eastern Europe. And it was his work with the Society that became the subject of collaboration between Moss and Schubert in early 1918.

In early 1918, the Krakauer Society was staging a benefit concert to raise money for (as Moss described them) "the poor Jewish people of the East Side," and Moss asked Lee Schubert to donate the use of one of his theaters for the event. Schubert informed Moss that, alas, he could not do this, but

---

3 Readers interested in the sordid details should see *Mr. Broadway*, the autobiography of Gerald Schoenfeld, the lawyer-turned-impresario who redeemed the Shuberts' theatrical empire after the founders' presence had passed from The Great White Way.

he would be happy to donate a hundred dollars to the cause. The Society expressed its gratitude for the donation and booked the Shubert Theatre at the established rate of $250. The event went forward without incident on March 17.

A few days later, Moss opened his mail and found a bill from a Schubert Theatre manager for production "extras" amounting to $96.99. Moss was shocked at the idea that the Shubert organization would try to claw back Shubert's donation in this way; and so he paid the bill, assuming that a mortified Lee Shubert would pay the money back to the Krakauer Society once he'd been notified that his underlings had acted in this way. But Lee Shubert insisted on full payment, along with an additional surcharge of $10.50 (for expenses not specified in the correspondence).

"This bill for extras was paid without question," wrote Moss in a letter dated April 23, 1918. "I had not the slightest doubt that the matter would be immediately adjusted when it was brought to your attention, because I cannot conceive that after you volunteered to contribute $100.00 to a charity, you would take it back through various added charges . . . Legally, the Society would not have to pay for extra help already included under [the $250.00] contract; but there is no thought on our part of entering into any legal squabble. In fact, after having prided myself with the members on securing your aid [for the event], I would prefer to shoulder the [financial] burden personally—as in the case of the enclosed check—rather than ask the Society to pay and thus confess that in my enthusiasm I had been mistaken."

This prioritization of reputation and rectitude over money and power was a constant in B.S. Moss's life. Long before the idea of "corporate social responsibility" became popular in the late twentieth century, he partnered with a stream of charities, and lent his stature to progressive political causes. Moss's approach to business arguably cost him fame and fortune during the gold-rush days of the film industry. It also laid the foundation for a sustainable family-owned brand that, built up on the basis of reliable behavior and sound business judgment could survive intergenerational transition, not once but twice (and counting).

The sort of power that B.S. Moss seemed to care most about was the kind that a man applied internally to police his own impulses. Indeed, he said as much to his son Charles in letters they exchanged, which also set out sensible if sometimes mundane strategies for living a happy and productive life.

* * *

By the late 1920s, B.S. Moss seemed to be on his way out of the entertainment business. He was in his mid-fifties. He had started with nothing, built an enormously successful business, raised a family, made a comfortable home in Manhattan and supplemented it with a summer place in Far Rockaway. He was devoting more of his time to community affairs and politics: in 1928 he was chairman of the Advisory Committee of the Curtis-for-Vice-President Club, the purpose of which was to attach Senator Charles Curtis of Kansas, a chief proponent of equal rights for women, to Herbert Hoover's Republican ticket. The Republicans, at the time, were seen as more progressive than Democrats on social issues. B.S. Moss got his wish: Curtis was selected as Hoover's vice-president, and he would make his first campaign speeches at Moss theaters in New York.

Around the same time, B.S. Moss participated in a wave of consolidation sweeping the film and vaudeville theater companies. The Stanley Company of America and the Keith & Orpheum vaudeville circuits were combined with the Moss theaters into a new company that would represent over 600 theaters in the U.S. and Canada and employing some 15,000 vaudeville performers. It would eventually be rolled into RKO Pictures, a division of the Radio Corporation of America, or RCA. The company was worth an estimated $250 million and touted as "the most powerful unit of the amusement industry" in America.

Moss had effectively retired, but not for long. As always, the entertainment industry was a dynamic field, with new talent, new shows, growing audience expectations, and new technologies. It was one of the latter that seems to have given B.S. Moss something of a second wind.

* * *

The rise of the "talkies," motion pictures that projected their own sound, is traced to the 1927 Warner Bros. film *The Jazz Singer*, which dazzled audiences with its synchronized recorded musical score and sequences of recorded speech. In truth, the end of the silent-film era unfolded over several years, and had several false starts before silent films became obsolete. In the 1920s, RCA pushed a system it called Photophone. Moss's old fur-bench friend William Fox promoted something called Movietone. As early as 1923, a system called Phonofilm, invented by Lee de Forest and Theodore Case, was in use for the production of short films. But the major studios eventually settled on the Warners' system, then known as Vitaphone, which had demonstrated proof-of-concept in the 1926 film *Don Juan*. Even by this late stage, however, Jack Warner, often credited as the talkies' original visionary, believed that the new technology would be used mostly for music and sound effects, and that dialogue would continue to be communicated to audiences in the form of printed text.

As competing technologies rose and fell, exhibitors struggled to rewire their movie houses with speakers and other sound equipment. In some cases, orchestra pits were removed and replaced with more seats. In other cases, the theaters were abandoned entirely in favor of new constructions. In his 1988 book, *Hollywood and the Box Office, 1895-1986*, media-studies scholar John Izod reports that "the cost to the theater operator of Vitaphone equipment installed by Western Electric was to range between $15,000 and $25,000" per theater. Exhibitors serving small markets struggled with the capital outlays required to keep up. Even for many of the large chains, the timing was terrible, as it coincided with the onset of the Great Depression.

Moss was dazzled by the possibilities of talkies. In 1930, it was announced in the *New York Times* that he would construct a chain of from forty to fifty theaters specifically designed for talking pictures, the first of these to be built in Manhattan, with the largest costing between $1 million and $2 million each (the Great Depression would dramatically reduce the number of theaters actually built). Moss had hired Eugene De Rosa as architect in addition to a score of acoustic experts with instructions to ensure the interior of each theater was equipped with soundproof, non-absorbing walls, floors and ceilings, and seats arranged in the pattern of a fan to best line up with sound waves from the front of the house. Speakers would be distributed throughout the theater to permit a consistent reception of voices and music in every seat, and to eliminate echoes and dead spots.

Talking pictures cannot be successfully presented in houses where hard walls and balconies, protruding ornamentation and hard floors and seats combine to hurl back a distracting discord of sound repercussions," said Moss. "The talkies must have their own houses, completely sound-proofed and constructed in accordance with the fundamental acoustical principles with which modern science is now thoroughly acquainted."

It wasn't a total abandonment of vaudeville. The new theaters would have stages because audiences still expected some live entertainment with motion pictures. But Moss's business acumen is on full display here. The first significant talkie was released in October 1927. Within a matter of months, Moss was in discussion to unload his chain of old-style theaters. It would have been little more than a year later that he began formulating plans for purpose-built talkie theaters. Among the new properties would be the Criterion, the Moss company's flagship until 1999, built at the intersection of Broadway and 7th Avenue at a cost of $2 million.

To understand the importance of movies as commercial products during the middle decades of the twentieth century, it is important to consider the extent to which sound technology transformed the medium. Studios' newfound ability to let audiences hear the actors didn't just expand the methods by which stories could be told. It fundamentally changed the *type* of stories they could tell. The experience of film-going became more immersive, which in turn pushed exhibitors to create darker, quieter, more tightly controlled environments. As Izod explained in *Hollywood and the Box Office*:

> The long-established dominance in Hollywood of narrative over other forms of film was massively reinforced by access to dialogue. Now characters could be understood to a depth that had been unattainable even by the finest actors when expression of their meanings was limited to gesture, expression and the title card. Thus, the hero of the silent film, the character as type, is soon succeeded by the hero of the sound film, the character as psychologically distinct individual. It is a fundamental

change which allows the feature film to follow and in certain ways rival the novel in its familiar concern with the individual as the center of larger actions. This is more than a matter of theme and aesthetics alone, for it enables the feature-film industry to anchor itself even more deeply in the largest of all genres, that part of the market devoted to story and character . . . Sound not only subtilized narrative, it also let it move faster. The delays for reading title cards vanished; dialogue began to crackle; and the effect of offering a self-containing illusion (towards which Hollywood films had long been tending) was much enhanced . . . Spectators had little leisure to do more than react emotionally. Contemplation while the film ran became impossible, and cinema moved closer to becoming an engulfing experience.

The need for exhibitors to economize during the Depression years changed the viewing experience in more mundane ways, too. In the 1910s and 1920s, showmen such as B.S. Moss had filled their movie houses with the trappings of old-world grandeur, in hopes of attracting the most respectable (and free-spending) strata of society. But now that the cinema had become a mainstream entertainment medium and art form, such frills were extraneous. The armies of ushers that had once monitored the aisles were let go. Some found jobs in the newly erected concession stands, a sideline that would once have been déclassé at upscale movie palaces.

This latter innovation was especially important given that Hollywood's studio oligopoly was doing everything in its power to maximize its box-office take at independently run theaters. No matter what percentage the studios took from ticket sales, the exhibitor was guaranteed to get every cent of the concession profits. Of course, studios noticed what was happening and increasingly demanded and enforced minimum admission prices to prevent exhibitors from using bargain admission prices as a means to maximize sales at the concession stand.

While the economic fortunes of film exhibitors would rebound massively during World War II, with some theaters staying open twenty-four-hours a day to accommodate the shift workers now pumping out war matériel in American factories, this shift in the basic film-exhibition business model would be permanent. By one estimate, concession sales now account for about 40 percent of profits for American film exhibitors.

While the business of film exhibition has gone through many changes, the late twenties and early 1930s brought a sea change in the development of film exhibition and mass entertainment generally. Not only were talkies sweeping away silent films, but color would soon begin to push out black-and-white. For the first time, Americans began to view entertainment celebrities as a familiar, year-round presence in their lives whom they could see and hear. And yet another new medium had emerged to compete for the attention of the masses. In 1922, there were 75,000 Americans listening to radio sets. By 1928, that number was 35 million, about 30 percent of the country's population.

And all of this was taking place at a time when older entertainment forms were stubbornly refusing to leave the stage. As late as 1931, B.S. Moss's Broadway Theatre at Fifty-Third Street and Broadway (formerly the Colony) was presenting a program called "Varieties." As an article in an industry publication put it, the show consisted of "big time Vaudeville and Talkies." There were live performances by Ginger Rogers and The Albertina Rasch Girls (a ballet troupe) along with a showing of *Murder at Midnight*. The writing was on the wall, of course: an article in *Variety* just a few months later indicated that the Albertina Rasch girls had been fired as part of cost-savings moves that would "reduce the [weekly] stage overhead to around $5,000 for acts . . . about half of what Moss had been spending [previously]."

Yet even as Moss was presiding over the twilight of vaudeville, he also helped usher in a still another new medium that would eventually eclipse even film and radio in American culture. On October 13, 1931, he sent out a letter to the entertainment press and potential advertisers alerting them that "commencing Saturday, October 24, there will be presented at the Broadway Theatre for the first time on any stage and in the form of popular entertainment, a technical demonstration of television." Moreover, it was announced that a 30-minute segment of this new "television" technology would be incorporated into the usual "Varieties" fare at the Broadway Theatre, with real-time moving-picture images carried "by wire" from a real-life theatrical production in progress at the Guild Theatre on West Fifty-Second Street.

Louella Parsons, the famous and widely read entertainment columnist, attended the event and reported of the television experience that "the materialization was dim and nebulous as that at a séance. I'm not quite sure I would have recognized my best friend." She had a point. The projected image had a resolution of just forty-five horizontal lines, a tiny fraction of the 1,080 lines that are standard on today's high-definition sets. But technically, this was real television.

It is unlikely that most of the audience members at those 1931-era shows at the Broadway Theatre appreciated the historic nature of the spectacle, representation the transition from live performance, the most ancient of all entertainment media, to new technologies that would bring the 500-channel universe into every home. But as a news account illustrates, Moss understood that the crude prototype he was putting on display was just the beginning of something big: "This short television program, Mr. Moss pointed out, is not the debut of full-fledged television entertainment, but rather in the nature of an experiment. It is comparable to the nickelodeon stage of the movies. It is probable that in a few years, we will look back at the television playlets at the Broadway Theatre as . . . quaint forerunners of a mature art." Prophetic words.

And Parsons, for all her carping, agreed. She predicted in her review that this new thing called television "will be greater than all of the discoveries of this wonderful, unprecedented age. Then the peoples of the entire world may look in upon a play broadcast from the television studios of Hollywood . . . Cameramen of the future will have had their apparatus set up right at the scene of the then current Chino-Japanese disturbance, and scenes of carnage will be shown on the world's screens at the very second of their occurrence . . . Time and space will be annihilated . . . The world will have no room for secrets. And perhaps that isn't so good, either!"

Parsons, incidentally, also got a few things wrong. In a final flourish, she opined that "I cannot see why the perfection of television will have any adverse influence on theaters . . . There will, perhaps, be a few who have television sets in their own private projection rooms . . . But the multitudes will flock to the theater for their entertainment . . . We'll all be older before we say 'Let's go to the tellies tonight.'" For film exhibitors, that day would come all too quickly.

By his later years, B.S. Moss had developed a reputation as both an innovator and one of the industry's wise old souls. Reporters often asked him for his opinion on the state of film. Sometimes, he wrote articles on this subject under his own byline, as he did in the February 19, 1941 edition of *The Exhibitor*. At this point, the United States was still almost a year away from joining the war effort, and demand for film was flat. But Moss didn't blame the hard economic times for the lean revenues. Instead, he argued, the industry was pumping out formulaic fare and showing them in run-down theaters. "A couple of years ago, the motion picture industry, as a whole, spent over a half million dollars in a contest, the slogan of which was 'Motion pictures are your best entertainment.' This was a complete failure. The policy of 'The public be damned' . . . has done more to drive away patrons than anything else."

B.S. Moss had always been relatively high-minded about the quality of films he wished to show. In this latter phase of his career, he became more explicit about this project. In 1938, he began promoting the U.S. exhibition of upscale French films through a company he'd formed called Empress Pictures. Two years later, in an article in *Variety*, Moss noted that film could have a powerful social and even political role once World War II had ended. "Millions in Europe will be left destitute; drives to aid them will again be organized as after the previous war," Moss wrote. "[Movie] pictures can perform a great service . . . They offer a method of acquaintancing [the population] with the things they need to know to preserve their health . . . Let them show the people how pneumonia can be cured, how to put roses into the cheeks of their children, how to life themselves out of depression and despair."

In 1942 and 1943, thanks to the wartime boom, annual per capita movie-ticket sales peaked in the United States at around thirty. Soon thereafter, they fell precipitously, down to about twenty by the end of the decade. A 1949 profile of Moss noted that the "crushing throngs during the lush war years" had been replaced by a "vast yawn," and that Moss was now one of the few owners "ringing up a dollar happily while other exhibitors perished along the way." In too many cases, the public had begun "to throw ropes around the wallet and stay home to catch puppets, wrestlers, ball games and similar gauds on eye-straining screens called television." As Louella Parsons might have put it, viewers were saying, "Let's go to the tellies."

In 1946, Americans were spending $1.30 on movies for every $1.00 they spent on radios, televisions and records. Over the next decade, a period in which the percentage of electrified American homes with a television increased from 12 to 86 percent, and spending on movies dropped to 30 cents per person. As economist Stanley Ornstein noted in a 2007 analysis of the history of film exhibition, *Motion Pictures: Competition, Distribution and Efficiencies*, the high birth rate that followed World War II ate into the leisure time of many adults who often found it easier to stay home watching television than to hire a babysitter and attend a movie. Moreover, "people moved in large numbers to the suburbs, away from the (then) main concentration of downtown movie theaters." To the extent there was growth during this period, it lay with the drive-in niche, which allowed mom and dad to watch a movie while junior slept in the back seat.

From the studios' point of view, the rise of television was not much of a problem. They produced content, regardless of whether it was shown in theaters or on television. But for exhibitors, every customer who gave up the movie house for a smaller screen was a dead loss.

Regardless, B.S Moss persevered into the 1950s and continued to innovate, as well. One of his inspirations was that there was more to sell in a theater lobby than popcorn and soda. When filmgoers at The Criterion attended the premiere of the original 1951 adaptation of *Alice In Wonderland*, they were greeted by a novel sight: a pop-up retail store of tie-in souvenirs. A trade-journal article on this new experiment describes the "intriguing vista of another profitable by-product of theater operation." The Criterion had hired two live models dressed in *Alice* costumes to attract guests to the merchandise counter. An accompanying photo of the lobby shows a pop-up kiosk called the "Kiddie Korner," and a sign inviting children to enter the theater's "Do You Look Like Alice?" photo contest.

On the last day of 1951, shortly after *Alice In Wonderland* was first screened, the following item appeared in the *Brooklyn Daily Eagle*:

> Benjamin S. Moss, movie pioneer and owner of a chain of theaters in Long Island, Manhattan and New Jersey, died last night at his home, 983 Park Ave., Manhattan, at the age of 7[6]. Death follower a heart attack on Sunday.

The article outlined his contribution to the history of the theater business, including his tenures as president of the Vaudeville Managers Association and the Vaudeville Managers Protective Association. It disclosed that he had late in life become something of a real estate mogul, forming the Forest Hills Realty Corporation, the Polk Realty Corporation, and the Cedarhurst Construction Company. He was survived by his wife, Estelle, his daughter Beatrice Crystal, and his son Charles B. Moss, to whom this narrative now turns.

CHAPTER FIVE

Mallomars and Blockbusters

THE MERCHANDISING INNOVATION that marked B.S. Moss's last years in the business can actually by credited to his son, Charles B. Moss, who had taken a larger role in the family business as his father pulled back from his creation. By 1950, Charles was managing the Criterion and simultaneously looking after day-to-day operations of the entire Moss circuit. Lou Gerard gives this account of another of his pioneering involvement in movie tie-ins:

> The story begins properly about one year ago [in late 1950], when the Criterion booked a reissue of *Pinocchio* for its Christmastime attraction. Managing Director Charles Moss believed that *Pinocchio* merchandise could be sold, at least to some degree, in connection with the engagement, and turned the project over to the theaters advertising and publicity director, Jerry Sager. There was very little time for what was frankly an experiment . . . Sager contacted the Walt Disney character merchandising division and obtained the names of the manufacturers who had put out *Pinocchio* items. These he contacted by mail and in person . . . At the end of the engagement, there was practically nothing left over, and there was a very neat, completely new and unexpected profit on the ledger.

To a modern movie studio, for which tie-in product rights represent a major line item in the expected profits of any big-budget film, the idea of an individual film-house owner going out and procuring his own themed merchandise for retail sale may seem quaint. (By way of comparison: when STX released the 2019 animated movie *Ugly Dolls*, they assembled a list of 100 promotional partners including McDonalds, Carl's Jr. and Pinkberry.) But the only theater that sold *Alice in Wonderland* merchandise when the movie was released was Charles B. Moss's Criterion in Times Square.

Raised on Manhattan's Upper East Side, Charles B. Moss was a studious child, eager to please his parents and, like his father before him, focused diligently on self-improvement. These qualities eventually would be rewarded by his admission to Cornell University. Among the few surviving documents from his early life are long, handwritten lists of vocabulary words and phrases he sought to memorize: *panacea, ubiquitous, halcyon, picayune.* He was nevertheless known to have a boyish side: his friends referred to him as "Buster," because his haircut resembled that of the Buster Brown shoe character. His mother called him "Buddy." He was addicted to Mallomars, the chocolate marshmallow treats. Because the chocolate on Mallomars tended to melt, they weren't sold in the summer, so Charles would buy a huge supply every spring to get him through the warm months. (His addiction to Mallomars and supply management techniques would be adopted by his son, Charley.)

Charles always had a close relationship with his father. He was said to idolize him. The surviving correspondence between the two is not extensive and somewhat formal in tone, which was not unusual for the time, but its content demonstrates a warm and healthy relationship. In one particularly interesting letter to the teenaged Charles in 1932, B.S. offers advice on how to keep slim. He prescribes a regime of "gym at 12 o'clock, a few games of handball, shower etc. all completed by 1 o'clock. [But] please understand that nothing is accomplished in this old world of ours without hard work."

Cornell offered Charles a fine opportunity for intellectual exploration. While there, he noted the communist agitation at play in many parts of the world and wrote a detailed and admiring portrait of the Russian Revolution and the Soviet system of government. He described it as "a great laboratory of life . . . a people daring enough to believe that there is something greater than private profit."

Charles Moss also wrote at least four plays at Cornell, one of which, *This Is What Happened*, won the university's $100 annual prize for best original one-act play on an American Theme in 1934. He also directed the work of other playwrights, including *The Bracelet* (1910) by Alfred Sutro. A surviving sheaf of papers among his university materials contains detailed handwritten notes on the staging of the production, including diagrams of how characters would move about the dining-room set.

His intellectual interests belied the conservative social instincts Charles had inherited from his philanthropic, community-minded father. The plays he wrote at Cornell were respectable comedies of manners, not revolutionary tracts, and his interest in socialism seems to have been confined to academic papers. He joined the (primarily Jewish) Pi Lambda Phi fraternity as an undergrad, acted as business manager for the university's *Freshman Handbook*, and served as associate manager for the student newspaper.

Charles Moss graduated from Cornell in 1934, in the teeth of the Great Depression. He managed to find a role for himself in the entertainment business consistent with his artistic interests. An admirer of the European film, again much like his father, Charles got a job selling movies for the British unit of France's Gaumont Film Company. Unfortunately, the company soon went bankrupt.

Charles next found work making radio and television shows. He produced the long-running quiz show *Quick As a Flash* and Mickey Spillane's *Mike Hammer* radio and TV series.[4] He eventually signed up with another east-coast film circuit and learned the ropes of theater management and eventually followed in his father's footsteps as manager of the family's flagship, the Criterion. He never abandoned his artistic interests, however. In fact, in Charles B. Moss's first appearance in the *New York Times*, he is

---

4 In the Moss archives is a rejected script furiously scribbled over by a displeased Mickey Spillane, whose final comment to Charles B. Moss was, "This stinks," accompanied by a doodled image of a toilet.

identified as the executive director of the Criterion and the new purchaser of the Fifty-fifth Street Playhouse, which he would extensively refurbish and re-open as an art house devoted to first-run showings of quality foreign films.

When Moss stepped into his role as manager at the Criterion, he seems to have inherited all the goodwill that his father had earned over three decades in the business, and then earned as much again on his own account. Upon meeting a young Charles, one veteran of the industry wrote that "it is a very pleasant stick of candy in life to revere a man and then find out that his son is all right, too . . . The sons of Broadway somehow never quite fit their feet into the footsteps of their fathers. The exceptions are to be counted on about two small fingers. One is very definitely Charles Moss . . . Moss is no giddy scion of entertainment. He thinks seriously."

As B.S. Moss receded into the background, Charles became the public face of the company at commercial events. Published photos of Moss the elder from this period typically are confined to charity galas or stock publicity. When the Mosses launched a big film, Charles was front and center. When the family opened a bowling alley in Forest Hills, Queens, in 1942, it was Charles who appeared, with wife Paula, in hammy publicity photos that show them bowling two balls down the same lane. The two had been married in 1938 at the Hotel Pierre in Manhattan. The daughter of Mrs. Arthur. C Mendelsohn and the late Mr. Mendelsohn, the bride had attended New York University and Columbia College. The couple's honeymoon, according to the *Brooklyn Daily Eagle*, took them to Florida.

Like his father, Charles became well known to the general public, thanks mostly to his appearance at film premieres at the Criterion. The *Daily News* featured him in their regular feature, "The Question." In one instalment, perhaps an early test of the strength of his marriage, he was asked for his opinion on the truth of Margaret Mitchell's words in *Gone With the Wind*, "No wife ever changed her husband one whit." Moss's answer: "I do agree. A wife may influence her husband's conduct, but . . . she can never change his basic characteristics."

Picking up on his father's use of television to captivate visitors to his theater, Charles in 1949 installed in the lobby of the Criterion a new Tradiovision TV set with a then-massive four-by-three-foot screen, which the newspapers referred to as "life size." The stunt, marking the Criterion's thirteenth anniversary, was designed to underscore its reputation as "the theater of tomorrow." Three years later, Moss installed a $25,000 "movie-size TV screen" at the Lee Theater in Fort Lee, New Jersey, to broadcast a New York Metropolitan Opera House performance of *Carmen*, more than a half century before live broadcasts of opera in movie theaters became commonplace throughout North America.

Behind the scenes, Moss, like everyone else in the film exhibition industry, was struggling to meet the long-term challenge posed by television. There were positives to the new medium: it could be used to promote movies and celebrities and keep people lining up at theaters in the same manner that newspaper entertainment reporters and gossip columnists had done earlier in the century. There was no denying, however, that it convinced a portion of the office to consume entertainment at home.

Moss's conclusion was that he needed blockbusters to compete. As he later told a *New York World-Telegram and Sun* reporter, "the business was changing . . . the day of the small picture was ending. Only big hits could survive." And the success of his approach was reflected in the title of newspaper articles with headlines such as "Criterion Grows on Moss: Owner Gambled on 'Big' Films; Now Greenbacks Fill Till."

Leveraging the fact that the Criterion was a great venue for movie premieres, Moss bet on big motion-picture properties that would not only fill his seats on opening night but keep them coming back for weeks on end. Starting in the 1950s, the long engagement replaced a high turnover in films as the basic business strategy for theater managers. Newspaper stories and newspaper advertisements began noting that a film such as Burt Lancaster's *Brute Force* was being held over for its seventh week, breaking the all previous records at the Criterion. Several years later, Danny Kaye's *Hans Christian Andersen* packed them in for nine weeks. By the end of the decade, it was not uncommon for a film to last several months. *The Ten Commandments* opened at the Criterion in November 1956 and was still playing in March 1958, seventeen months later. And even then, it was bumped only to make room for another long-running blockbuster, *South Pacific*. Longevity had become a prime measure of a film's popularity.

* * *

In 1963, Charles Moss travelled to Los Angeles with his teenaged son, Charley Jr., for a series of meetings with film executives, the most important of which were at the Warner Bros. lot in Burbank. The purpose of their mission was to compete for major film openings, which were conducted at a small number of handpicked theaters across America. Negotiations for openings were often conducted in person between distributors and exhibitors. Among the distributors, none was more powerful than Jack Warner, the fifth surviving son of a Polish cobbler who'd fled Europe's pogroms around the same time as B.S. Moss's own parents.

This was also a family reunion of sorts. At the time, one of Warner's executive assistants was Steven Trilling, a nephew of B.S. Moss, a cousin of Charles B., who owed his original entry-level position on the Warner Bros studio lot to an intervention by B.S. Having climbed the ranks into Jack Warner's inner circle, Trilling now was the studio president, the number two person on the Warner lot, with a leading role in managing its production pipeline. There were few better jobs in America. Trilling was Hollywood royalty, and he lived the stereotypical life of a Tinseltown big shot, moving casually within the town's celebrity circles, always getting the hottest tickets and the best table.

When Charley and his parents paid a visit to Trilling's beautiful modern home in Holmby Hills in 1963, they were shocked to bump into none other than the singer and actor Frank Sinatra, who was using Trilling's driveway to store a white Buick Riviera convertible with a big pink bow that he'd bought as a surprise birthday present for his ex-wife Nancy.

"You know Frank, don't you?" said Trilling casually to his guests, impressing Charley forever.

Charles S. Moss was after one particular film on this trip to Los Angeles: the screen adaptation of *My Fair Lady*, which would star Audrey Hepburn and Rex Harrison. It was the talk of the entertainment world, the biggest Hollywood production of its time. Everyone in the industry (correctly) believed it would be a massive hit when it hit screens the next year. It represented a potential bonanza for the Criterion: the arrangements that then governed the industry not only gave particular theaters a right to display hit movies for months on end, but they were given the film exclusively in their region, allowing them to draw audiences from a whole metropolitan area. That generated heavy profits for exhibitors, much like a hit Broadway play.

Jack Warner was a feared and imperious figure in Hollywood, and he often treated his subordinates disrespectfully. Especially Trilling. "If Jack wanted to play tennis at 11 p.m.," remembers Charley Moss, "Trilling's phone would ring. It didn't matter what time it was. Steve did what Jack said." At the Warner Bros. executives' private dining room, there was a special spot reserved for Jack at the head of the table, with the vice-presidents clustered at the other end, separated by a bunch of empty chairs that no one was allowed to use. Everyone rose when Jack walked in, as if he were a judge or state governor. He would then spend the whole lunch taking calls on a phone that had been installed under the table for his personal use.

Charles B. and Charley Moss accompanied Trilling to the *My Fair Lady* set, specifically to the library of academic snob Henry Higgins (played by Harrison). Later, while the grown-ups talked business, Charley was taken by a studio publicist on a lot tour during which he had his photo taken, holding a prop revolver, alongside actor James Garner, dressed in his *Maverick* cowboy getup. Meanwhile, Charles S. and Trilling hashed out the terms under which the Criterion could play *My Fair Lady*.

Then as now, exhibitors' deals with studios worked off something called a "split." For a small-town theater, this might typically mean that in the first week of exhibition, the theater would pay the studio 35 percent of gross receipts, 30 percent for the second week, and 25 percent on all subsequent weeks. But the structure of these deals was different in big markets such as New York City, where the potential profits were much higher. A typical arrangement at first-run urban theaters during this era was a so-called "ninety-ten" deal, with the studio getting 90 percent of the take, and the exhibitor left with 10 percent. This nominally lopsided ratio is deceiving, however, because the exhibitor took a fixed, pre-negotiated amount off the top, before the 90/10 division of proceeds, to cover "house allowance" overhead: payroll, heating, electricity, insurance and so forth.

In theory, the exhibitor's 10 percent take was a reliable measure of the exhibitor's profit, since his costs had been covered up front. But these negotiated "house allowance" overhead estimates proved to be an elastic concept. The expenses would be grossed up to include both direct expenses incurred during a film run and more ill-defined general and administrative (G&A) "soft costs" such as home-office overhead and executive salaries, which were referred to as "water." The quantity of water included in any deal often was the subject of vigorous negotiation.

For example, consider a 90/10 deal on a theater with a $20,000 house allowance, grossing $100,000 per week on a film. This would yield $28,000 for the exhibitor (i.e., the $20,000 house allowance, plus 10 percent of the remaining $80,000), with the remaining $72,000 going to the studio (90 percent of $80,000). If the $20,000 house allowance were a true reflection of the exhibitor's expenses, his profit would be $8,000. But if the $20,000 house allowance contained, say, $5,000 in water, the actual profit would be closer to $13,000.

There were other ways to play the game. In the mid-1970s, Charles B. Moss's single-screen, 1,540-seat Criterion operated with a set house allowance of $18,500 per week. But when the Criterion was "twinned" (i.e., divided in two), each of the two smaller theaters were assigned a house allowance that was only slightly reduced—$16,500, or a total of $33,000 for the two screens. So the arrangement yielded $14,500 more house allowance than under the original $18,500 single-screen arrangement. Thanks to the economies of scale that come from operating multiple screens under the same roof, the associated weekly expenses went up by only about $3,000. That amounts to an extra $11,500 profit per week. Eventually, the studios got tired of this system and ratcheted down house allowances to the extent the market permitted. ("They basically said to us, 'Lower your house allowance or I'll just play the film down the street,'" Charley recalls.)

At the time of Charles B. Moss's pursuit of *My Fair Lady,* the film was on track to be one the most expensive ever produced, and Warner Bros. was determined to make back its money even if the movie was a flop. Trilling told Charles that he would be required to put up something new: a "guarantee," a sort of reverse house allowance that locked in a minimum return for the studio. To help this go down easier, the studio offered a more favorable split. This kind of guarantee-based deal offered exhibitors a bigger upside if the film was a hit, but also required them to shoulder the loss if the film bombed. In effect, the studios were off-loading risk onto downstream partners, a strategy they would pursue more systematically in the latter decades of the twentieth century, as bankers began asserting themselves more in the business of film production.

In the case of *My Fair Lady*, the guarantee that Trilling demanded was $1.25 million. The number stunned Charley's father. It felt to him like the studios were trying to offload *all* of their risk onto downstream partners. *My Fair Lady* was a much-ballyhooed film, but it wouldn't have been the first out of Hollywood to fail to live up to the hype. If it failed and the Mosses were left holding a $1.25 million guarantee, their business would be in big trouble.

Charles didn't agree to Trilling's terms until he'd returned to New York. He analyzed the expected return on investment and worried himself almost to death before finally feeling assured that the risk was worth taking. It ended up being the right call. *My Fair Lady* was a huge hit. The reviews were stellar, audiences were enthusiastic, and the movie's production budget of $17-million was dwarfed by a $72-million box office. It also cleaned up at the 1964 Oscars.

The decision to ante up for *My Fair Lady* was something of a turning point in the career of Charles B. Moss. Not only did the film pay direct financial dividends at the ticket booth, but along with *The Ten Commandments* (1956), *South Pacific* (1958), *Lawrence of Arabia* (1962) and *Funny Girl* (1968), it entrenched the Criterion as one of New York's few truly elite venues. The luster associated with such designations would fade in the 1970s and 1980s, as moviegoing became an increasingly suburban experience, and studios eschewed exclusive arrangements in favor of a national wide-release distribution strategy. But until then, this kind of prestige helped the small Moss circuit punch above its weight in competing with larger chains.

An unfortunate coda to the 1963 Los Angeles trip involved Steven Trilling. Jack Warner's stepdaughter Joy Page, an actress best known for her role as a young Bulgarian woman in *Casablanca*, was married to William

Orr, a talented studio executive whom Warner was pushing up through the organization. Trilling, despite his long and loyal service to Warner, began to get pushed aside.

In January 1964, a few months after the Mosses had visited him on the Warner lot, an unhappy looking Trilling had his picture in the papers alongside Jack Warner and Frank Sinatra, who was holding a shovel, breaking ground on a new $500,000 Frank Sinatra Building at Warner's Burbank Studios. It was the kind of attention Trilling usually received. He had a top job at a powerful studio, but he wasn't a headliner: he was "also in the picture," as when he'd served as a pallbearer for the producer Michael Curtiz along with Cary Grant, Alan Ladd, Danny Thomas, and Jack Warner.

The Sinatra ground-breaking was one of Trilling's last public acts for Warner. He soon lost his job. As the *Los Angeles Times* reported in February, "Warner told Steve Trilling he'd give him a new contract when he got back from New York. As soon as Jack left town, another exec gave Trilling the axe." He may have been Hollywood royalty, but at the end of the day, Trilling was someone else's employee, and an expendable one. His wife, a horse-track addict, had already had left him for a jockey. Their daughter was enmeshed in a succession of tawdry sexual affairs. Alone and unemployed, Trilling killed himself. It was another tragic Hollywood ending, but not tragic enough to get a paragraph in the local papers.

For such a powerful behind-the-scenes figure, Trilling remains a surprisingly obscure figure in Hollywood lore. His funeral, and who attended it, did not interest the press so it is impossible to know whether Jack Warner bothered showing up, or if the news of his long-time assistant's death even registered with him emotionally.

* * *

Steven Trilling wasn't the only Moss family connection to the Warners' founding brotherhood. Another came through Jack's brother, Harry Warner, who remained a bachelor until the day he set eyes upon a *Ziegfeld Follies* performer and former child-actor named Lina Basquette. He was a 37-year-old Jewish Romeo to her 18-year-old Catholic Juliet. They tied the knot on Independence Day, 1925, two years before Warner died of complications arising from a mastoid infection. Basquette, whose beloved father had committed suicide when she still was a child, became a widow at the age of twenty-one, and a single mother to Harry's child, a baby girl named Lita Warner.

Unlike other actors from the 1920s, Basquette managed to extend her stardom into the age of talkies.[5] In later years, she traveled the world as a live performer, and even met Adolf Hitler when she worked as a contract actor for Leni Riefenstahl. (Basquette claimed that the future Nazi leader made advances on her, but that she rebuffed him with a knee to the groin). After World War II, she began a long career as an award-winning breeder of Great Danes. A 1993 *Washington Post* profile portrayed her as an energetic octogenarian and dubbed her "the grande dame of Great Danes." Technically, her film career lasted seventy-five years: in 1991, aged eighty-four, she was cast in a small independent film called *Paradise Park*, her first role since 1943. But her personal life carried the Hollywood curse.

When Harry Warner died, the surviving Warner brothers, who'd never accepted Basquette into the clan, feared baby Lita would be raised Catholic and so offered Basquette an extraordinary sum to surrender custody. In a moment of weakness, she acquiesced, but then spent agonized years trying to reverse her decision in the courts. Before she died in 1994, Basquette would have another child (a son), attempt suicide at least twice, get raped by a soldier during the Second World War, and embark on eight more marriages, the last to a man nineteen years her junior (it ended after three days when she realized he was gay.) She would also reconnect with her daughter Lita, although not until 1993.

---

5   Lina Basquette's most famous movie was a noble flop called *The Godless Girl*, a 1928 Cecil B. De Mille-directed melodrama in which the young actress starred as an atheist activist (Judith) who embraces Christianity after falling in love with the leader of a Christian youth group (played by B-list Western actor Tom Keene). In the climactic scene, whose filming has become the stuff of Hollywood legend, Bob helps Judith escape from a burning prison, and the pair ride off together into a bright Christian future. To achieve maximum realism, De Mille burned down the real film set, but bungled the job, and almost killed several of his actresses in the process. Basquette lost her eyebrows in the blaze, and they never grew back entirely.

Lita's own life was less eventful, but far happier. She had a comfortable childhood, attended Stanford University, and developed a passion for horses and bullmastiffs. Her first marriage, to a doctor, didn't last long. But her second, to a real estate developer and financier named Mort Heller, would last until Heller's death fifty years later. She passed away in May 2019. An obituary in *The Aspen* Times reported that this "well-known philanthropist and entrepreneur" was survived by three children, and by two stepchildren from Mort Heller's first marriage, one of whom, Robin Heller, would change her name to Robin Heller Moss in 1972, when she married Charley Moss, son of Charles B. Moss, and grandson of B.S. Moss, in the Florentine Room at the Carlton House on New York's Upper East Side.

Given the tragic arc of Basquette's first marriage, one can only imagine how she regarded the prospect of becoming stepmother-in-law to another film producer. But, according to Charley, the thought of history repeating itself never crossed her mind. "We got along famously," he remembers. "She and her husband Mort were truly my second parents, and part of the reason that we bought a home in Aspen. I was able to see her within a month of her death, and she was just as elegant and regal at ninety-two as she'd been when I met her."

CHAPTER SIX

The Boys in the Booth

I
N 2000, THE INTERNATIONAL ALLIANCE of Theatrical Stage Employees (IATSE) published an obituary for "Brother Steve D'Inzillo," a farm boy turned film projectionist whose career in union politics may stand as one of the longest in the history of organized labor. First elected to the executive board of New York's Local 306 in 1938, D'Inzillo remained in that post for the next sixty-two years, except for the period when he volunteered in the Air Force during World War II. One intriguing episode mentioned in his obituary directly concerns the Moss family.

A man of social conscience, D'Inzillo took it upon himself to "rehabilitate 25 convicted criminals" by finding them honest employment within the union. "All but two of the ex-offenders became productive members of Local 306," it notes. But "one of the two men who was not successfully rehabilitated assaulted Brother D'Inzillo in the Local 306 office." As it happens, that assailant was a projectionist at the Criterion in Times Square, the Moss flagship theater.

The Mosses had taken on this hard-luck case at D'Inzillo's urging. In the 1960s, the days when the projectionists' union was a force to be reckoned with, and for an exhibitor looking to stay on the right side of his workers, a favor of this nature might pay for itself in any number of ways.

Unfortunately, the new hire didn't prove to be a team player in the projectionist booth. Shortly after beginning work, he became so enraged at a co-projectionist that he grabbed the poor innocent by the ankles and dangled him out of a second-storey window on the back side of the Criterion. No one got hurt, but Charles B. Moss was understandably outraged. He immediately told D'Inzillo to get the charity case off his property. Even in the rough-and-tumble world of Local 306, defenestration was deemed an inappropriate technique of conflict resolution technique, and D'Inzillo complied.

Angry at this outcome, the ex-con next stormed the Union 306 offices, found D'Inzillo and brutally assaulted him, a misdirected act of retribution for what the projectionist imagined a case of unjust dismissal. The details of the crime, like the assailant's identity, are lost to history. But this was no casual punch-up. According to the IATSE obituary, "Brother D'Inzillo suffered the loss of his left eye."

For ordinary victims, this would be a hugely traumatic, life-defining event. Amazingly, D'Inzillo didn't even mention it in his memoirs, which are preserved in the archives at Columbia University.

Of the many types of employees required to operate a theater, from ticket takers to popcorn servers to ushers, none is more vital to the enterprise than the projectionist, without whom the show literally won't go on (technology has since made the exhibition of film a much simpler process). For much of the Moss family's history, employing projectionists meant dealing with Steve D'Inzillo and his union. D'Inzillo's extraordinary story bears telling here not only because it supplies an important blue-collar counterpoint to a narrative otherwise told from management's perspective, but because his life intersected directly, and fatefully, with the Moss family.

D'Inzillo was a tough nut from a young age. The union boss was born three years before Charles B. Moss, about five miles distant, in markedly different circumstances. He was one of eleven children inhabiting an apartment on Bleecker Street in Greenwich Village, then a hardscrabble neighborhood near the heart of the garment district. (The gunshot that almost killed B.S. Moss outside his ill-fated Knickerbocker Cloth Examining and Shrinking business would have been within the D'Inzillo family's earshot.) In the 1910s, as B.S. Moss was embarking on a career as entrepreneur D'Inzillo's own father moved the family out to a farm in Bound Brook, New Jersey.

There, D'Inzillo milked cows and tended livestock. As a nine-year-old, he often would be sent into town to sell the farm's peaches and pears at 35 cents a bushel.

Before long, D'Inzillo quit school to help support his family. Like a young B.S. Moss, he sold newspapers. In his teens, he took a job at a chandelier factory, bending and shaping the metal arms that held the light bulbs, and worked at the docks unloading banana boats from Central America. He learned the reality of class struggle through the "great laboratory" of hard knocks. The chandelier factory fired him when he joined the union. On the docks, meanwhile, it was the union stewards whom he feared. "When you answered the shape-up," he said, referring to the daily union-run process of picking workers, "you didn't get picked unless you gave a percentage of your salary to the right people."

Again like B.S. Moss, D'Inzillo migrated to the entertainment industry. He found employment at the Senate Theatre in the Bensonhurst neighborhood of Brooklyn. His official job title was Reel Boy and Assistant Superintendent. But as D'Inzillo remembers, he did "every conceivable job in the theater," from tending the coal-fired boilers, to ushering, to cooking and washing dishes. At the age of sixteen, he became the theater's projectionist. In the modern era, that means pressing a button on a computer console. During the interwar period, film projection still was delicate tradecraft. D'Inzillo was so good at it that he got hired back for jobs even after he'd fallen out with the union.

The Senate Theatre, he recalls, had "two simplex machines with a multi-generator set and rheostats with dimmer boards in the booth." Their operation was analogous to that of a car with a manual transmission. Long movies required five or more film reels, and the projectionist had to change the reels over every twenty minutes or so, which could be accomplished without interruption only by ensuring that the next reel was queued up on a second projector while the running projector spooled out. If done properly, the audience would barely notice the changeover, much like a smooth gear change in a stick-shift car: "You had a clutch and when you started the motor, the motor would run, and the open parts of the clutch would turn. Then you would let out the clutch handle itself, which would slowly press the two clutch plates against the disk that was on the driving shaft of the projector. That way the projector would start up slowly and pick to speed. You had to become expert enough that you wouldn't make the [film] changeover until it was up to speed to match the outgoing projector."

As at his previous jobs, D'Inzillo fought back at what he regarded as corrupt, strong-arm tactics exercised by both management and unions. As a result, he fell afoul of a notorious labor leader named Sam Kaplan, who leveraged his position as a means to push sales to his own projector company. When one of Kaplan's lieutenants demanded a $200 payment for a union membership card, D'Inzillo balked.

For a while thereafter, he worked as a mechanic at a boat club, where he saw "how the other half lives." From the docks, he saw Howard Hughes and his yacht, *Southern Cross*, "often with at least three, four, or five gorgeous women" on board. One particular assignment that stood out was changing the bathroom exhaust in the master bedroom of a yacht belonging to socialite Tommy Manville (an inheritor to an asbestos fortune, whose thirteen marriages to eleven women once earned him an entry in the *Guinness Book of World Records*). "We go into the bathroom and there's armed guards. Why? The fixtures in the toilet were gold."

During this time, D'Inzillo remained on his union's blacklist. But the leaders of Local 306 eventually turned a blind eye when theater owners hired him on as a needed technical trouble-shooter. These were the days when some theaters still ran their electric power off generators that couldn't serve two projectors simultaneously for more than a minute or two before blowing out. Coaxing these machines back to life was an art form D'Inzillo had mastered.

Eventually, he also proved his worth as an organizer during the strikes and infighting and mob infiltration that rocked the industry during the 1930s. By the time D'Inzillo came back from military service, he was Local 306's vice-president and Business Representative, in which capacity he spent the rest of his career, staring across negotiating tables at men such as Charles B. Moss, who by now had graduated from Cornell.

At its peak in the 1940s, Local 306 had, by D'Inzillo's count, about 2,450 members. There was a political edge to its activities. Local 306 sometimes collaborated with the Young People's Socialist League and similar (long-defunct) groups that eventually would become the focus of a McCarthyite backlash after World War II (a movement that would have an especially important impact on the film industry, thanks to the House Un-American Activities Committee's special focus on Hollywood, and the notorious blacklist that emerged in its wake). D'Inzillo, like other prominent labor leaders, often found himself being denounced as a communist.

As time passed, however, Hollywood's Red Scare petered out. Unfortunately for D'Inzillo, so did his profession. The fifties and sixties brought challenges for both owners and workers alike. With the onset of television in the early 1950s, about 40 percent of New York's movie theaters closed. Some 450 projectionists were thrown out of work in the space of a few years.

By 1966, Local 306 finally had become the single union representing projectionists in New York City, but it was a pyrrhic victory for D'Inzillo. Exhibitors were learning to do away with the old system of having a projectionist present a feature-length movie by chaining together 20-minute reels. Instead, films could be spliced together in one big horizontal "platter" that could be played all at once. Employers, D'Inzillo noted, no longer felt a projectionist was essential. "There are many theaters operating without full-time projectionists," he said. "Union as well as non-union. . . . There are a lot of places where even the cashier is trained how to thread up, how to make splices and all."

With few cards to play at the negotiating table, D'Inzillo recounted, "we [tried] to base our argument mainly on the sociological aspects . . . It's very elementary that the more people who lose out, regardless for what reason, the larger the unemployment segment of society, the less the purchasing power of all consumers. That reduces the demand on the productive capacity, so the entire business machinery either stops of begins to go backward."

In his 1974 negotiations with Moss and other theater owners, D'Inzillo proposed "that we would undertake to give them a free hand in eliminating jobs without restriction, provided they would give us a lifetime guarantee of either employment or wages in lieu of employment." Not all union leaders of the era were so realistic or accommodating. And for a time, union contracts imposed bloated staffing requirements on theater chains. The Criterion itself employed four projectionists for a booth that required only one, as well as four stagehands for a building with no stage. Regardless, they had come to terms without any of the vitriol and violence that characterized labor relations at the time.

* * *

That D'Inzillo and Charles B. Moss found common ground says something about each of them. The projectionist turned union leader, while a man of strong principles had an important pragmatic streak. There is no other way his career could have spanned from 1926, when he got his state projectionist's license in 1926, through the twilight of the silent era, the golden age of the talkies in the 1930s and 1940s, the industry retrenchment of the 1950s and 1960s, the mechanization and suburbanization of theaters in the 1970s, and the first stages of the digital era we inhabit today.

As for Charles B. Moss, he was as conservative in his business dealings as he was in his life. He ran the family business in a professional manner, adhering to conventional corporate standards and structures. He was calm, measured, and understated in everything he did, an approach that permitted durable alliances and good relations with all of his stakeholders.

Even his hobbies were conservative. According to a short biography composed after his death by his wife Paula, "he was an avid collector of antique British clocks and watches, which he was capable of repairing when necessary. He also collected British wool-embroidered portraits of sailing vessels, stitched by the sailors during their long voyages at sea . . . He had a penchant for sophisticated cameras and developed and printed his own photographs."

But there was something unusually broad-minded in Moss's conservatism, and it was rooted in his strong sense of community. Throughout his career, Charles raised funds for an array of film-industry charities, such as the Will Rogers Memorial, the Motion Picture Pioneers and the Variety Clubs of New York (a tradition taken up enthusiastically by his son Charley and grandchildren Ben and Liz). This was in addition to his roles in the

Jewish community. As a young man, Charles helped create a new synagogue in Scarsdale, and in 1956 he chaired the Entertainment Committee of the Federation of Jewish Philanthropies, much as his father had helped lead the United Jewish Appeal's relief effort for Jewish refugees in the lead-up to Israel's creation in 1948.

That same sense of community, of taking responsibility for the welfare of others with whom you live and worship and so business, informed Charles B. Moss's approach to labor relations. There is no doubt that unions created headaches for him, and not just Local 306. Unionized projectionists, for instance, refused to cross another union's pocket lines. They wouldn't play a film that wasn't certified by the International Alliance of Theatrical Stage Employees (IATSE), which required that everyone on the credit roll be unionized. In practice, this often meant that studio executives would simply write a check to the IATSE for their sign-off, even if the credit roll contained non-union names. It was effectively a union-imposed surcharge on the film-going experience.

Moss had little choice but to play along. The first job of a theater manager is to keep the doors open. But he was clever about it. There were two classes of movie theater in the Broadway district. The first-tier ones were required by their unions to employ four projectionists. The second-tier theaters were allowed to operate with two, making their operating costs lower. However, when Charles had an opportunity to lease and operate the second-tier Forum on Broadway and 47th Street, the union said he would have to employ four projectionists: he owned a first-tier theater so the union attributed the first-tier model to everything he owned. Charles developed a plan.

The Guild Theatre on Broadway and 50th Street was a tier-two outfit. Charles went to its owner, Norman Elson, and offered to be a 50 percent silent partner if Elson were to purchase the Forum. A deal was struck, and it later expanded to encompass other properties, including a three-screen theater up the block. Charles, a large, big-boned man, and the slight Elson would have lunch once or twice a week at the Friars Club. Elson would usually be on his first or second scotch by the time Charles arrived, sometimes along with Charley. It was a great relationship. When Charles decided to make a quadplex out of his wholly owned Criterion, he brought Elson into the bargain because it was bound to upset the competitive dynamic for film exhibition in the district. "They never looked at their contract for the fifteen years they were together," says Charley with admiration.

Notwithstanding his occasional maneuvers to avoid the excesses of the unions, Charles was careful to treat their members and their leadership with consideration. It was on this basis that he and Steve D'Inzillo developed a long, cordial, and respectful relationship, although their interests weren't always aligned. Both sides also managed to communicate that respect down to the next generation.

Although Steve D'Inzillo never made it to college, his daughter Jane graduated from Cornell, Charles Moss's own alma mater, and became a psychiatrist. At Cornell, Jane met her husband, future film producer Bill Badalato (*Top Gun, Alien: Resurrection*), who developed great admiration for his father-in-law. "Steve not only knew his craft, he understood the ramifications of his craft within the industry itself," says Badalato. "Many union leaders know what's going on in the union hall, but not in the outside world. Steve understood technology. If he were born in a later age, he would have been a computer wiz."

Badalato remembers the esteem with which his father-in-law and Charles B. Moss regarded one another, and it was through this relationship that Bill met the third-generation of the Moss dynasty in the 1960s. At the time, Bill was the production manager for a division of Columbia Pictures called EUE/Screen Gems. He became Charley Moss's first boss in the movie-production business.

Steve D'Inzillo's obituary recognized the work he did on behalf of America's projectionists. The success of Local 306, it said, "is mostly due to its tireless and visionary organizing drives, and it can be safely said that nobody worked harder, with as much success, as Steve D'Inzillo. Brother D'Inzillo was responsible for the outreach efforts that secured contracts with every major cultural institution in New York City utilizing motion picture and/or audiovisual facilities."

He should also be remembered for his insight into some of the fundamental problems that developed in the American economy during the latter half of the twentieth century. D'Inzillo understood that the hollowing out of New York City's projectionist trade in the postwar decades stands as a sad microcosm for the city's decline during this period. The rich stayed rich, but decamped for life in the suburbs. Meanwhile, the working class lost whatever job security and social status once were associated with a skilled blue-collar profession. The sort of men who once might have supported an entire family on the wages earned in the projectionist booth were forced to subsist on piecemeal, minimum-wage jobs. Much has changed in New York since the 1970s, but that basic problem of haves and have-nots encoded in the career arcs of Moss and D'Inzillo persists to this day.

D'Inzillo's concern for the plight of projectionists seems prescient in today's era of rising income inequality. While well-educated, well-capitalized entrepreneurs such as Charles Moss were free to pick and choose their markets and business strategies, the same wasn't true for the men D'Inzillo represented, whose only real asset in life was training in a field for which demand had evaporated.

CHAPTER SEVEN

Welcome to Times Square

ON THE GETTY IMAGES WEBSITE, under the title "WS POV Traffic on Broadway at Night," is a captivating two-minute snippet of Warner Bros. stock footage shot out of the rear window of a car traveling southbound on Broadway between the mid-Fifties and Forty-Second Street. It's 1962, the same year that the Criterion set a record by charging moviegoers the then-astonishing $4.80 to see *Lawrence of Arabia*.

This was an era when many people still dressed up to go to Times Square, which was full of glitzy theaters and nightclubs that had their names spelled out in neon on the Getty Images video: Jack Silverman's International; Birdland: Jazz Corner of the World; the Roseland Ballroom (which was then featuring the Buddy Bair Orchestra and Ramon Argueso). A block further south comes Lindy's (whose cheesecake would be celebrated in *Guys and Dolls*), and Tony Canzoneri's Paddock Bar and Grill. (By this time, the famed boxer had already died, and the bar was under the control of an up-and-coming Genovese-family gangster named Anthony "Fat Tony" Salerno.)

As of this writing, Manhattan is down to just one single-screen commercial movie theater: the 581-seat Paris.[6] But in the early 1960s, movie
palaces were still abundant on Broadway. As the car passes Fifty-First Street
in the video, one can see the Loew's Capitol Theatre, playing the *Gunga
Din* remake *Sergeants 3* (known to film historians as the last movie that
featured all five members of the original Rat Pack). Opposite is the Winter
Garden Theatre, which was then playing Mel Brooks' musical football farce
All American.

A few second later, the Rivoli comes into view, with *West Side Story* advertised on its enormous marquee. Sitting across the street is the Trans-Lux,
which even in this age of television was still offering viewers newsreels and
shorts: *JFK Visits with Ike, Bloodshed in Algiers,* and *Cartoon Travelogue Comedy:
African Big Game*. Then the car moves into the upper Forties, and we glimpse
the Warners' Theatre, showing *El Cid*, the Forum (*Satan in High Heels*), the
Victoria (*The Day The Earth Caught Fire*), the Astor (*The Children's Hour*) and
the Loew's State (*The Four Horsemen of the Apocalypse*, an epic MGM bomb
that appalled reviewers and audience members in equal measure).

The car stops at Forty-Fifth Street for a red light. Once it starts up again,
we can see the Criterion Theatre on the left, featuring *Walk on the Wild Side*,
a racy film noir about a group of New Orleans prostitutes (one of them
played by a young Jane Fonda). Alongside the theater are Woolworths,
Regal Shoes, and a handful of other shops. On the second floor sits the
venerable Bond clothing store, home of the famous "two trouser suit," its
signage extending the entire length of the block, and then curling around
onto Forty-Fourth Street at which point it shares the video frame with
the Paramount on the west side of Broadway, with *Madison Avenue* on the
marquee. Finally, as we get to Forty-Second Street, comes the Rialto, whose
marquee provides a foreshadowing of the fare that will stain Broadway's
brand in the years to come: "*No Time For Shame*: For Mature Adults Only."

---

6   Interestingly, the Paris Theater, after closing at one point in 2019, was purchased by Netflix
    which, in turn, hired Bow Tie to manage the theater. Whether it will be used exclusively for
    Netflix content or exhibit other films has yet to be determined.

The degradation of Times Square in the early 1970s was the backdrop to the popular 2017 HBO television series *The Deuce*, the title being an old byword for the area of Forty-Second between Seventh and Eighth avenues. But the process actually began earlier, in the mid-1960s, when operators already were installing 25-cent peep shows in some storefronts. In 1968, the Loews Capitol was demolished after presenting *2001: A Space Odyssey* as its final run. The Trans-Lux was turned into a porn theater, as was the Rialto (although it eventually would become the site of a recording studio, used by Geraldo Rivera and Montel Williams, before being torn down in 2002). The lobby of the Forum became a delicatessen. The Astor was shut down in 1982 to make way for the Marriott Marquis hotel. The Paramount was turned into office space. The Warner, Rivoli and Loew's State all were demolished in 1987, the latter site becoming the home of the 44-floor Bertelsmann Building, which sits across Forty-Fifth Street from the Moss family offices. Even Broadway's live-theater industry seemed in peril, its future being secured only thanks to Gerald Schoenfeld and Bernard Jacobs, who rescued the floundering Shubert Organization with the stunning success of *A Chorus Line*, which they brought to Broadway in 1975.

It wasn't just Times Square that was suffering in the seventies, of course. White flight, the oil shock, racial unrest, fiscal management, rising crime rates and the general collapse of blue-collar manufacturing in New York City all had conspired to repel tourists and transmit urban blight. But Times Square was hit especially hard, as its appeal had relied on an aura of refinement and high-end cachet. "My dad had always made people line up outside the theater rather than wait in the lobby," says Charley. "He would always say people want what they can't have, so if a movie looked like it was difficult to get into, that made them want to see it more." But no one wants to line up in a crime-ridden area inundated by men whose only mission was to spend fifteen minutes in a dark room. Moreover, as *The Deuce* conveyed, even a legalized triple-X exhibition industry tends to bring with it a low-end criminal ecosystem of pimps, drugs, and organized criminals.

Yet not everybody stood opposed to Times Square's transformation into a sexualized playground. The Stonewall riots, a series of impromptu, violent demonstrations in favor of gay rights, took place in 1969. New York's first gay-pride events took place the next year. Despite an unsavory reputation (homosexuality was still illegal in most of the US), businesses providing X-rated gay entertainment formed a key part of the social hub that bound a whole cohort of gay men who'd come to the metropolis seeking friendship, sexual liberation and an escape from homophobia, and helped to forge the pre-AIDS-crisis gay culture of the 1970s and 1980s in New York and other large cities.

One of the interesting aspects of pornographic film exhibition during the 1970s was that, in these early days of sexual liberation, it wasn't yet established trade practice to firewall porn off from mainstream film. For a brief time, there was even a fashion for middle-class couples to go to risqué movies together on dates. Some of the Manhattan theaters Delany describes were dedicated porn spaces, but others went through periods when they would mix in triple-X films with mainstream fare. At the Variety Photoplays theater at Union Square, for instance, management used color-coded tickets to signal to customers what was on the screen, with porn on Tuesday, Thursday and Saturday, and regular fare on other days. The porn itself often seems to have been a random mix of straight and gay fare. (Oddly, Delany notes that the gay regulars would show up no matter what kind of porn was on offer.) As late as 1978, when the Mosses were developing a multiplex property in Yonkers, a *Herald Statesman* reporter felt it necessary to note that the Moss family would not be showing "hard-core porno films" in their "new, ultramodern MOVIELAND 1, 2, 3, 4 theater complex," as this, apparently, would not have been an unprecedented business practice.

* * *

New York City always has had a unique role in the history of film exhibition. But the land-use arc traced here of old movie palaces transforming to office space or other retail uses, often going through a porn phase as an intermediate step, played out across many large North American urban centers. The famed Princess Theatre on Third Street in Milwaukee provides a representative example. Operating as The Grand in 1904, it boasted the city's first Edison Kinetoscope projector. The Princess flourished in various upscale forms until World War II, when it was gradually relegated to B movies under the ownership of a New York-based chain called National General. In the 1960s, adult movies were added to the mix, and a passageway was built to an adjacent nightclub so that customers could enter the theater without revealing themselves as porn enthusiasts. The property eventually fell into decay. (One of the universal aspects of porn theaters is that owners typically invest literally nothing in infrastructural upkeep, on the proven theory that no amount of dinginess can repel a dedicated customer.) In 1984, it finally was demolished, with little fanfare or notice, and replaced with a parking lot.

In smaller towns and rural areas where people are more easily recognized by friends and family, fewer theaters were repurposed for X-rated content. Consuming pornography in the company of others always has been something people do only at the furthest ends of the intimacy spectrum, either in front of complete strangers, or with close sexual intimates, but rarely in the company of casual acquaintances, neighbors or co-workers.

As part of the hollowing out of Main Street America that took place in the latter Cold War years, single-screen theaters in small markets usually closed down, with local demand being mopped up by massive suburban multiplexes that catered to regional markets. And the few that remained in operation—a good example here is the Leavitt Fine Arts Theatre in the vacation town of Ogunquit, ME—tended to survive as passion projects subsidized by local entrepreneurs or arts organizations, or were repurposed as live-event spaces.

In many cases, small-town American theaters retained a faded dignity even as their audience increasingly abandoned them for the multiplex or stayed home watching videotape rentals from Blockbuster. They stood and, in scattered cases, still stand as churches of American cultural nostalgia for the generation of Americans that gave us *Happy Days* and kids-on-bikes movies such as *E.T.*

Artist Davis Cone's hyper-realistic paintings of traditional movie houses line the walls of the Moss offices, and many are reproduced in a 1988 book by Linda Chase, *Hollywood on Main Street: The Movie House Paintings of David Cone*. His depictions of 1980s-era theaters are charming and sentimental, but often with a hint of melancholy. One 1985 piece, for instance, portrays the venerable Knox Theatre in Warrenton, GA, sitting lifeless beside a gas station, with the heartbreaking title on the marquee reading, "*Seems Like Old Times*, with Goldie Hawn." Along with old churches, schools, fire stations and department stores, these buildings housed the civic soul of traditional town life, which is why it can feel sad, even at the artistic distance afforded us by Cone's work, to observe them in their twilight.

In many cases, the attachment that people felt to their town cinema was based on practical considerations, as theaters had civic functions apart from their commercial purpose as exhibition spaces. For teenagers too young to drive, they often provided the only spaces that were consistently available for (quasi) private romance. They provided entry-level employment opportunities for high-school workers or retirees. And, in some cases, they were used as shelters during emergencies, roles for which they were well-suited as the whole architectural purpose of a movie theater is to admit rapidly large crowds and provide them with a comfortable, serene, hygienic, and orderly environment.

"One year, there was a big fire in one of the buildings near the movie theater—I want to say it was the late 1970s," remembers Sandy Moran, whose grandparents once ran the Playhouse in Larchmont, New York, which subsequently became part of the Bow Tie Cinemas. "My grandfather was a volunteer fireman . . . and he ran over there and opened up the theater and made it a safe haven for those who lived near the building that was on fire . . . For New Year's Eve and Christmas Eve, my grandma would cook and bring him food and they would set it up downstairs. People would come in to see a movie and then have something to eat, especially those who had nowhere else to go . . . For everyone who worked there, it wasn't just a job; it was a place where everyone socialized and took care of each other."

PHOTOGRAPHS

1

3

4

B.S.MOSS' BROADWAY   B.F.KEITH'S HAMILTON

MEZZANINE-B.S.MOSS' REGENT   B.S.MOSS' REGENT

INTERIOR
B.F.KEITH'S
JEFFERSON

LOBBY
B.F.KEITH'S
JEFFERSON

INTERIOR
B.S.MOSS'
FLATBUSH

5

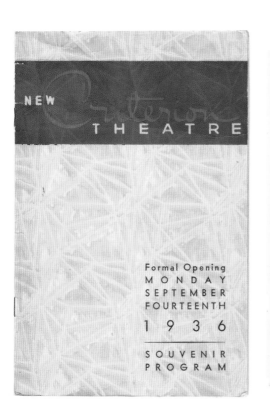

NEW *Criterion* THEATRE

Formal Opening
MONDAY
SEPTEMBER
FOURTEENTH

1936

SOUVENIR
PROGRAM

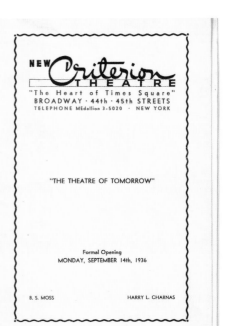

NEW *Criterion* THEATRE
"The Heart of Times Square"
BROADWAY · 44th · 45th STREETS
TELEPHONE MEdallion 3-5020 · NEW YORK

"THE THEATRE OF TOMORROW"

Formal Opening
MONDAY, SEPTEMBER 14th, 1936

B. S. MOSS   HARRY L. CHARNAS

The Theatre of Tomorrow

Top center, Auditorium, looking from stage. Indirect lighting throughout, also tone-control booth (upper right). *Right center*, Grand Lounge or "Green Room". Carpets, drapes, wall paper and furniture are all in restful green. *Upper right corner*, Promenade, rear of orchestra. Soft carpeting in tones of tans, browns and restful reds. *Upper left corner*, The entire sole nymphs invite you to enter, relax and enjoy yourself. The color designs are silver and gold, with carpets and lighting blending into a blaze of color. *Lower left corner*, Right Mural panels executed by Lembke. *Lower right corner*, Left Mural panels executed by Lembke. *Left center*, Ladies Lounge and Powder Room, in restful tones and intimate furnishings.

6

7

8

9

10

11

12

13

14

17

18

19

20

21

22

23

24

25

26

27

28

CHAPTER EIGHT

Location, Location, Location

U NLIKE THE OTHER GRAND movie houses of Broadway, which had been falling like dominoes, the Criterion was still around in the mid-1970s. The theater was even the subject of a lively looking two-page spread in *Hollywood on Main Street* (although by the time Cone painted it in 1986, the Criterion already had been chopped up into a six-plex). But behind the brightly lit marquee, the business was in trouble, and there was a real risk that this flagship Moss family cinema, which had been in continuous operation since 1936 and which, even in its humbled state, did as much business as its other five theaters put together, would fold and die along with the building that contained it.

In one sense, the fact that commercial rents had bottomed out in Times Square was a plus for the Moss family, since Charley and Charles had a smaller check to write to their commercial landlord, the Bond Clothing company, every month. But they also knew that the situation wasn't sustainable for the property owner, and that eventually the property would get flipped to a new buyer who would repurpose the property, probably to build another skyscraper, and let the Criterion follow the Loew's State, Astor, Victoria and all the rest into the dustbin of movie-house history. That was the nightmare scenario that disturbed Charles's sleep. He spent a great deal of time looking for alternative buildings for the Criterion. At one point he even scoped out the Nathan's Famous Hot Dogs location down the street. He couldn't find anything that worked, which only added to his anxiety. Then Seymour Durst arrived on the scene.

Durst was a big-time developer who Charles knew socially. He had an ambitious plan to create a 10-acre Rockefeller Center-style office complex on the block bounded by Broadway, Sixth Avenue, Forty-Fourth and Forty-Fifth Streets. That required him to scoop up building after building. He bought Bond's building and became the Criterion's landlord. To finance that particular purchase, Durst had done a deal with the US Steel and Carnegie Pension Fund. The pension fund bought the property for $13 million and leased it back to Durst, who was busily trying to snap up other properties. The harder he worked, the more worried Charles B. Moss became about the future of his flagship theater.

As the economic morass of the seventies deepened, Durst got himself into financial trouble. He defaulted on his lease with the US Steel and Carnegie Pension Fund, and that organization took over the property and became landlord to its tenants, including the Criterion. Getting Durst out of the way might have been a relief for Charles but the pension fund seemed just as intent on developing the building and making back its $13-million investment.

As it considered its options, the pension fund acted as landlord at the property. Dealing with tenants in a challenged rental environment in a sinking economy was outside its skill set. The leases of several of its tenants all came up at once. Stubborn and inflexible, the pension fund lost all of them, including its anchor, Woolworth's. The Moss company and the Criterion were now the only ones paying rent, and reluctantly so. Charles had deputized Charley, who was now working full time in the family business, to negotiate a break on their monthly payment. That brought Charley into contact with Bob Wilson, the pension fund lawyer.

A white-shoe attorney at a white-shoe pension fund, Wilson was out of his element on Broadway but he and Charley got along, and the Criterion's rent was negotiated down to $1,000 per week. One advantage of being the lone remaining tenant in the business, was that Charley was able to build something of a lifeboat friendship with Wilson. The two men were soon playing the occasional game of squash. Over post game beers, Charley learned that the pension fund was trying to flip the building. It wanted its $13 million back and was marketing the property worldwide. Charley took the news back to his father, whose panic hit new heights.

Unfortunately for the pension fund, the global market for old buildings in run-down neighborhoods in a faltering economy was not strong. Meanwhile, the only tenants it had been able to attract were fly-by-night companies selling souvenirs and fake oriental carpets. Wilson, at wit's end, suggested that the Mosses acquire the building. Charley said they'd love to, and he thought $13 million was a fair price for a property in a world-class location, but his family didn't have $13 million. There things stood for months, the pension fund unable to find either good tenants or buyers. Charley eventually broke the stalemate in early 1978, somewhere between the office, the squash court, and the showers, by suggesting a compromise.

The property purchased by the pension fund consisted of retail space, the Criterion theatre, a gay pornography theater, and some single-room occupancy units, flop houses or bordellos. The only part the Mosses really wanted was the 204-foot strip of retail and entertainment along Broadway from 44th to 45th Street, through the bowtied knot of Times Square. "Why don't you just sell us the retail and our theater," suggested Charley over another post-squash beer, and find another buyer for the rest. Wilson was not enthusiastic but said he would consider it. He eventually came back to say he would let go the retail and the theater for $4 million. Charley said, "Four million might as well be thirteen million—we don't have it." The only way it might work, he added, is if the pension fund provided financing. Wilson agreed to lend the Mosses the whole amount, at 8.5 percent interest, with the first year's interest, $320,000, paid upfront, in cash.

When another potential buyer, one of the ex-tenants, expressed interest in buying the building on the same terms, the fund simply wrote up two copies of the sale contract and sent one to each buyer, instructing them that whoever got the signed contract back first would win the building. Charley and Charles were up all night with the contract. There were things they wanted to change, but in the end decided that none of these was significant enough to risk losing a good deal over. They hurried in their contract and wound up the winner. And a good thing it was: thanks to the explosive growth of the New York real estate market in the decades that followed, that single stroke of the pen probably created more value for the Moss family than every other one of their family business ventures put together, going all the way back to B.S. Moss's days as a cloth sponger.

One of Charles B. Moss's golfing buddies was Jerome Greene, a lawyer and developer who was one of the owners of the Carlyle Hotel. He admired the deal Charley had struck and invited himself in as a 25 percent partner, arguing that it would spread the risk and that he would bring some expertise to the mix. Charley was not keen, but his father thought that spreading the risk might be a wise idea. He also thought Greene could help them with tax issues. Greene was invited in, on condition that he waive any conflict-of-interest claim arising from the Moss's both owning the property and using it for their business.

Getting the best part of a $13 million property for $320,000 cash was quite a bargain, but Charles and his son hardly felt like lottery winners at the time: what they'd won was an empty building in which their own money-losing theater was the only occupant. "Really, I was just scrambling to find tenants who would help carry the taxes and the mortgage," says Charley. "None of the major retail companies would touch Times Square at the time." Between interest, taxes, insurance and other operating expenses, the building was losing over $20,000 a week.

They eventually managed to fill the space, and what mattered most in the long term was that the Mosses had purchased a piece of Times Square, sometimes called "the crossroads of the world." In a retrospective on Times Square published by the *New York Times* in 2004, architecture reporter David W. Dunlap described the east side of Broadway, between Forty-Fourth and Forty-Fifth streets, as the "crossroads of the crossroads; maybe its birthplace." It was the site where Oscar Hammerstein built the Olympia Theatre in 1895, almost a decade before the area (which was then called Longacre Square) got its name; where Florenz Ziegfeld, Jr. started up his Follies; and where, as Dunlap writes, the city's ageing vaudevillians staged their last real celebratory hurrah in 1935, shortly before their venue, the Loew's theater, was torn down to make way for the Criterion, whose own glory years stretched well into the 1960s.

It is easy to imagine that B.S. Moss, if he were still alive, would have been horrified to see the depths to which Times Square had fallen by the 1970s, and that he would have been ashamed to see his flagship Criterion chopped up into a multiplex and surrounded by scenes of blight. All the same, he would have adjusted quickly. During his own life in New York City, the patriarch had seen numerous neighborhoods rise and fall with the times. He had lived through the Great Depression and seen friends and family lose their fortunes (and lives). Moreover, the very reason that men such as B.S. Moss even lived in the United States was that their European homelands had been transformed apocalyptically by war and tribalistic hatreds. A little street crime isn't the end of the world.

B.S. Moss knew something else, too. It is the cycles of growth and decline that allow smart investors to profit from buying real estate and developing businesses in emerging markets. In some cases, those markets consist of virgin neighborhoods under construction, like the northern tip of Manhattan when B.S. Moss built the Coliseum a century ago. In other cases, as with Times Square in the late Cold War period, they consist of bad neighborhoods due for an upswing. Ironically, the muggers, porn peddlers, and drug dealers who were scaring away moviegoers from the Criterion were the same people who allowed the Mosses to buy some of the most valuable commercial real estate in the Western world for the same price that—in inflation-adjusted terms—would get you a smallish to mid-sized condo overlooking Central Park today. It's hard to imagine that B.S. Moss wouldn't be proud of that deal.

* * *

An interesting footnote to the purchase of what became the Bow Tie building involves the part of the property that the Mosses left with the pension fund. The back pieces, including the single-room-occupancy units, were sold to a slippery developer who owned several such buildings. Unfortunately for him, the city made it illegal to tear down single-room-occupancy buildings without a specific permit. The night before the new law went into effect, the developer brought in bulldozers and tore down the back of the building. He hadn't acquired the necessary permit. Nor had he bothered to turn off the building's electricity or its gas feed. "He might have blown up the whole block," says Charley. The developer was subsequently indicted, and got off with a fine.

CHAPTER NINE

The Horror Diversion

CHARLES B. MOSS HAD ENJOYED the advantage of methodically learning the field of film exhibition while working side-by-side with his father B.S. Moss over fifteen years. It was an orderly generational transition and a delicate balancing act, with the son collaborating respectfully with his father, he also challenging him to push the business in new directions to keep up with changing markets. Charles' son, Charley, would not be so blessed.

Charles died in 1979, nine days before his sixty-seventh birthday, leaving the 34-year-old Charley alone at the helm of the family organization. Some competitors, and at least one news reporter, wondered whether he was in over his head. Not without reason. The old adage about family money puts it this way: "The first generation makes it, the second generation spends it, and the third generation blows it." According to Family Business Institute statistics cited by the *New York Times*, the old adage is optimistic: "only about 30 percent [of family-owned businesses] survive beyond the founder's generation, and just 12 percent make it to a third." It would take many years before Charley definitively prove to naysayers that, like his father, he was "no giddy scion of entertainment."

Charley Moss was born on Manhattan's Upper East Side, not far from the Yorktown neighborhood where his grandfather was raised in the early twentieth century. In the 1950s, however, his family became part of that great suburban migration that hollowed out New York and dozens of other American cities. He spent his boyhood in Scarsdale, New York, a Westchester County bedroom community for upscale Manhattan office workers.

His homeless in Scarsdale was comfortable, but his parents' marriage was not particularly happy. Charley remembers his father as just another dad heading into the office every day, although it was clear he was passionate about his work. His wife stayed home and lived the life of a suburban homemaker. That she was often impolite, rude to the people who worked for her, and invariably late to events disturbed her husband, sometimes deeply. Charles would feel the need to take breaks from home life, disappearing for days at a time without notice.

When Charley asked his father why he did this, Charles responded with an illustration: "You know how rain barrels fill up, and water starts to run over—and sometimes you have to tip them over? That's kind of why I take those trips." It was a way to relieve tension without doing irreparable harm to the marriage. "He was never going to leave her," says Charley, who found his parent's discordant relationship disturbing. "So he needed those breaks."

Scarsdale High School, Charley's alma mater, produced a lot of bold-faced names in the early 1960s: Robert and Douglas Durst (whose real estate magnate father, Seymour, coached Charley's baseball team), Richard Holbrooke, Jeff Hoffman (one of America's first astronauts) and, briefly, Liza Minnelli (she never graduated).

Charley himself drifted through the school's corridors without much enthusiasm or distinction. By his own account, he was an indifferent, overweight student, and not much of an athlete. At DePinna, a Manhattan clothing store, his mother would take him to the "husky" department, as it was then called. Asked, while passing his old school's football field, if it brought back memories of glory days, he laughs and says if he'd been in the stands when anything glorious was happening, he'd probably have been too focused on his Hershey's bar to notice.

Every once in a while, Charley's schoolboy life would be interrupted by brief, glamorous interludes, usually corresponding to a gala opening of a blockbuster film at the Moss-run Criterion Theatre in Times Square. Family photo albums show Charley dressed in suit and tie, appearing with his parents alongside Bob Hope, Sophia Loren, or the famed Mexican comedian and *Pepe* film star known as Cantinflas (Mario Fortino Alfonso Moreno Reyes). In these photos, some of which now line the walls of the Bow Tie offices, Charles, with his trademark bowtie and pipe, appears friendly and serene. Charley's mother Paula, a beautiful woman who nevertheless felt like something of an ugly duckling in the company of Hollywood actors, presents to the camera with a broad but slightly nervous smile. Charley also seems out of his element, like an earnest but ill-at-ease child following a photographer's instructions at a wedding or bar mitzvah. They were familiar with red carpets, but they were not a natural habitat for the Moss family.

While many of Charley's classmates went to the Ivy League after graduation, the best Charley could do was a second-tier state university in the American south, where he found himself roomed with someone he remembers as a vocal anti-Semite. Motivated by this glimpse of where life would take him if he didn't work to his potential, he got his marks up and eventually transferred to the University of Pennsylvania, which became a launching pad for law school and his successful career as a film exhibitor. Charley Moss was a late bloomer.

While at law school, Charley had a fleeting brush with big-budget Hollywood filmmaking. The producer Howard Minsky was a family friend. He had asked young Charley about his plans and on hearing that he was headed for Boston University's law school, mentioned that he would be in Boston shooting a film called *Love Story*. He invited Charley to round up some campus extras to appear in the film. "He thought it would be fun for me," says Charley. "He was right!"

Charley wasn't paid for his efforts. He was merely having fun and helping out a film-industry veteran, and he didn't think much of it at the time. But the film those extras appeared in would go on to become the highest grossing movie of 1970 and turn Ryan O'Neal and Ali McGraw into major stars. It also would help eventually vault the cutthroat Paramount Pictures executive who handled *Love Story's* distribution, Frank Yablans, into the company's presidency, a development that later would have important ramifications for Charley's prospects.

Charley's first paid employment in the film industry was a summer job in 1969. He had already decided he didn't want to practice law. He wanted to go into pictures. His father called Steve D'Inzillo and enlisted his help. D'Inzillo's son-in-law was Bill Badalato who, although he had *Top Gun* in his future, was himself on the entertainment industry's lower rungs. Charley's entry-level position was a gopher at a Columbia Pictures' subsidiary that produced television commercials in New York. It was not an obvious choice for a fresh law-school graduate, but the role did teach Charley the rudiments of film production. And it made him a fast friend. Charley and Badalato hit it off and quickly realized they had the same ambition: to make a feature film. After securing financial support from Charley's father and a few other investors, that's exactly what they did.

To say that *Let's Scare Jessica to Death* began as a long shot would be an understatement. The original screenplay from which it evolved was called *It Drinks Hippie Blood,* more a send-up of the horror genre than an actual specimen. Charley had commissioned the script from a Connecticut writer and future Emmy-award winner named Lee Kalcheim, whose credits would later include mainstream TV shows such as *The Paper Chase, M*A*S*H,* and *All in the Family*. Kalcheim was going through a horror-farce phase at the time, having just written an obscure film called *Blood of the Iron Maiden*, in which, as IMDB describes it, "a crazed movie director gives LSD to aspiring actresses before murdering them with an iron maiden in his torture chamber." That movie flopped, and it's safe to say that *It Drinks Hippie Blood* would have done the same if it had been produced in its original form.

Moss was no expert at selecting scripts. But, like his father and grandfather, he often had a knack for spotting talent. The director he picked, an eccentric but brilliant up-and-comer named John D. Hancock, rewrote *It Drinks Hippie Blood* so extensively that it became a different movie, entirely stripped of farcical elements. As Hancock later remembered it, "I made it eminently clear to [Charley] that I did not want to do a satire of a horror picture. I wanted to do a movie that was legitimately terrifying."

Hancock decided to tell the story through the eyes of a woman slipping into madness while confronting the spirit of a drowned nineteenth-century bride, the cinematic equivalent of the unnamed governess at the center of Henry James' 1898 horror novella *The Turn of the Screw*. The result was a movie that spanned mainstream and art-house tastes. As film writer Michael Doyle wrote in a 2018 book, *Hancock on Hancock*, "with its delicately constructed air of growing unease and oppressive narrative that spotlights an emotionally vulnerable female protagonist, *Let's Scare Jessica to Death* has drawn . . . comparisons with Herk Harvey's *Carnival of Souls* (1962) and George A. Romero's *Night of the Living Dead* (1968)."

Hancock told Doyle he hadn't seen either movie at the time he made *Jessica*. He didn't have to. Many of the themes embedded in the film emerged not only from the early days of the horror genre, but from the great dark stew of American history and culture that, in the 1960s and 1970s, were beginning to assert themselves on movie screens. Like the ghost of Abigail Bishop emerging from the lake in *Jessica*, America's dark, wounded soul was being laid bare as part of the rebirth cultural historians call the New Hollywood or the American New Wave. Charley never set out to be part of this epic artistic experiment but, by good luck, he found himself with a lakeside seat.

Many of the most successful and memorable horror stories center on characters who are laid low by horrific discoveries after embarking on some fresh new phase in life. They are teenagers at prom, as in *Carrie*, or Jack Torrance at the isolated Overlook Hotel in *The Shining*, or lovebirds on an island retreat in *The Birds*. While the killing in these movies typically is done with knives, hammers, saws, and beaks, the true source of evil is oftenc presented as something that is lodged so deep within us that it cannot be defeated. Just as audience members expect will happen, the initial hope and joy is extinguished by a creature emerging from the unseen waters, mists, or darkness. Often, this act of extinguishing is metaphorically represented by someone who died in ancient times (almost always a woman or child), and whose miasma of guilt or suffering haunts the land and all who come near.

Hancock had barely entered his thirties when he began work on *Jessica*, part of the cohort of talented young directors who would transform American film in the latter decades of the twentieth century. At a 1974 Whitney Museum of American Art festival called "Hollywood's New Directors: Early Works," Hancock's early film about white-collar touch-football players in Central Park, *Sticky My Fingers, Fleet My Feet* was featured in the esteemed company of just four other directors: Martin Scorsese, George Lucas, Brian de Palma and Terence Malick. In keeping with the mood of America during the riots, assassinations and general cultural malaise of the Vietnam era, many of the emerging masterpieces of this period, like *Jessica,* were dark, violent and even nihilistic—*The Wild Bunch* and *Easy Rider* being oft-cited archetypes. Collectively, they represented a decisive rejection of the primary-colored moralizing and facile patriotism associated with the Motion Picture Production Code that had governed the industry until the 1960s. Like *Jessica*, these films featured morally (or even factually) ambiguous endings, and involved their audiences in the act of interpretation.

Jessica does not belong in the pantheon of American film classics. Rather, the whole thing was shot over only twenty-six days—a short production schedule for a commercial feature—and both Kalcheim and Hancock appear in the film's credits under pseudonyms (Norman Jonas and Ralph Rose, respectively). They were concerned that critics might see the movie as schlock which, indeed, a few did.

Even so, *Jessica,* the story of a mentally unstable woman trying to begin a new life with her husband on a haunted lakeside fruit farm, is not a turkey. Hancock was a disciple of Alfred Hitchcock, and successfully infused *Jessica* with many of the great suspense master's techniques, including, as Hancock would later describe, "the way Hitchcock retarded the pace in his pictures" so as to allow audiences to conjure the fear in their own minds before anything scary even appeared on the screen. The film starred veteran Tony Award-winning actress Zohra Lampert in the title role. Having played alongside Warren Beatty and Natalie Wood in *Splendor in the Grass,* she supplied the cast with credibility and name recognition. Plus, as Hancock would later recount, she was a "good screamer."

Jessica, to this day, is discussed by serious horror fans online. The film depicts the murderous ghost of Abigail Bishop coming up from the lake waters in the corporal form of a local drifter named Emily (played by

Mariclare Costello), dressed in Bishop's nineteenth-century wedding gown. The juxtaposition of deep evil and joyous innocence (the latter being represented in other horror films more often by a children's toy than a wedding dress) now is a well-established motif in horror films. It was more original and terrifying to audiences in the early 1970s, and it was patiently set up by Hancocks with seasonal atmospherics that appealed to filmgoers during this increasingly somber, inward-looking era of American art and politics. "I think the autumnal landscape can be read as a reflection of [Jessica's] psychology, or pathology, whatever you want to call it," Hancock says. "The fall is a time of death and decay in some ways, of natural change and disintegration, and there is a terrible beauty about all that. It helps us to understand that everything is finite: *Frail as the leaves that shiver on a spray, like them we flourish, like them, decay*, which is the poem on the grave rubbing that Jessica recites to Duncan and Woody in the car."

Jessica was shot in the old Connecticut towns of Old Saybrook and Essex in November 1970. Hancock remembers the sites as "gorgeous places to visit," full of apple orchards and pastures that inspired the film's emotional landscape. The *Handbook of Production Information*, which survives in Charley's archives, notes that the ageing fourteen-bedroom mansion in which the interior scenes were shot still contained the original stove and icebox dating from 1850.

Making *Jessica* was an exhausting grind, and one that Charley now remembers fondly, but there were tense moments when the whole production almost blew up. "We had a tight shooting schedule and a tight budget," says Charley. "We found ourselves behind schedule and over budget almost right from the start. I remember talking to my father and he said he thought we ought to shut the whole thing down before we lost a lot of money. It would be better for our investors, he argued, to lose a portion of their money than the whole amount. 'Better to lose a little than to lose a lot,' was how he put it. I was devastated because we were failing, and also because it was my Dad telling me this. Later I realized that it was probably harder for him to tell me than it was for me to hear it. But we eventually decided that if could hit our next benchmark in the production, we'd keep it going. And thankfully we did hit it."

There were also non-financial challenges. Costello and Lampert had to spend hours in the lake, shooting the swimming scenes. (No ordinary New Englander goes swimming in November.) The scene in which a soaked-to-the-bone Costello emerges from the water into the winter air was especially difficult, and one wonders how the actress managed to shoot it without shaking. Hancock himself had to do some of his work waist deep in the lake and remembers fish nibbling on him as he delivered instructions to the actors. Brilliant as he was, Hancock was still very green, and struggled to assert his authority over more experienced crew members. His first cameraman, a backseat driver, was fired during the first week.

Fights between producers and directors are the stuff of Hollywood lore, but Hancock seems to have had a great working relationship with both Mosses, and with co-producer Badalato, who would become a close friend. In *Hancock on Hancock*, the director described them all as "terrific producers to work with." He also remembers that the elder Moss was "clearly the guy in charge of things," despite being a largely "absent figure on set." Charley was the one who slept in the same hotel as the cast, got up early to the same bad breakfast, and ran around all day solving the numerous logistical issues that inevitably crop up when you're shooting a 90-minute movie in less than four weeks. In one case, he had to come up with a replacement for a mole that the script had *Jessica* adopting as a pet after finding it in a cemetery, but which died before its scenes were over. (They ended up using a mouse.)

Charley also ended up becoming deeply involved with the film's special effects, which pre-dated the modern use of computer-generated imagery. The production handbook specified, for instance, that one of the fake cadavers was to be simulated with "a mannequin obtained from a local department store window" stuffed with 150 ping-pong balls to ensure buoyancy. Moss and Hancock used their hotel swimming pool to design and test the system of concrete blocks and cables they used to control a mechanical dummy representing the underwater version of Abigail Bishop, an experience that Hancock says helped inspire some of his much bigger budget work on later movies such as *Jaws 2*.

As a producer, Charley had to do most of his work after the shooting was done. *Jessica* had to be packaged, promoted, and sold. This included the basic task of deciding what title to pick. In this regard, the decision by Paramount Pictures to rename *Jessica* (the working name used by the producers) as *Let's Scare Jessica to Death* was a masterstroke, serving to convey the possibility of the main character being not just the protagonist, but also the unknowing subject of some (possibly supernatural) experiment. And who is the person—or thing—proposing to "scare" Jessica? The ghost of Abigail Bishop? Jessica's own hippie housemate? The filmmaker? No one? The ambiguity isn't just creepy; it strikes a wry, self-aware tone while seeming to invite the audience in on a dark, mirthless joke.

Jessica had been shot on spec, without a distribution deal. This is where Yablans, mentioned earlier in connection with *Love Story*, returns to the picture. Charley knew him as the general sales manager at Paramount, the man who strategized and scheduled releases across the country. It was one of the very top positions in the firm. Charley managed to get him to screen *Jessica,* and he was impressed: "You guys must have spent half a million or more," he said. The budget had been slightly over $200,000. Paramount made a deal in the spring of 1971 to distribute the movie that summer. In the meantime, Yablans was promoted to the Paramount presidency.

For Charley, this was brilliant good luck, since it meant that the executive with the biggest office had a vested interest in mobilizing Paramount's resources to make the film a hit: *Jessica* would be the first release on his watch. Paramount was suddenly spending double what it would normally have laid out for the release of a film that size and picking up the entire tab. The Mosses did their part back in New York, pulling out all the stops when *Jessica* premiered at the Criterion. A horse-drawn hearse and prop coffins were set up outside the theater. The seats were packed. Ads that appeared in the New York press the next week boasted that the film had earned an impressive $32,128 at the Criterion during its opening three days.

Like other cult classics, *Jessica* is remembered more fondly now than when it was first released. A *New York Times* reviewer praised it as a "thinking man's vampire film," but also turned up his nose at the director's pursuit of "trivial shock effect." The *Los Angeles Times* similarly praised *Jessica* as a "realistic psychological drama," before declaring it undone by the supernatural plot devices that eventually emerge. For his part, though, Doyle notes that "some observers have commented in retrospect that *Let's Scare Jessica to Death* serves as a haunting elegy for the 'bitter disappointments of the Love Generation.' Whether by accident or conscious design, the film does effectively isolate and illuminate the death and corruption of counterculture values during the early years of the post-1960s hangover. It also anticipates the festering paranoia that was to manifest strongly throughout the 1970s in the wake of such events as the Watergate scandal, the assassinations of Harvey Milk and George Moscone, and the Jonestown Massacre."

Perhaps more significantly, Stephen King, in a 1992 interview, listed *Jessica* as one of his favorite horror films of all time. For fans of this genre, there may be no higher source of praise.

Although Charley didn't realize it at the time, he had gotten lucky with *Jessica* due to the fortuitous personal involvement of Yablans and Hancock, neither of whom involved themselves in Charley's next two films. These included *Stigma: The Curse That Begins With a Kiss*, an unusual 1972 mash-up between conventional horror and sex-education, in which an island town is consumed by the ravages of venereal disease until the heroes discover the dark secret and convince everyone to seek medical help on the mainland. Despite the unique premise, critics noted that the audio had been dubbed amateurishly, with spoken lines emitting from closed mouths. One wit opined in a scathing *Variety* review that the film "proves that boredom may also be a communicable disease." (The film was distributed on DVD decades later, but only because its popular young star, Philip Michael Thomas, would go on to play Detective Rico Tubbs on *Miami Vice* in the 1980s.)

Even after Charley's third film, *Diary of the Dead*, flopped in 1976, he was still looking to keep rolling the dice on new productions until a chance meeting in the outer office of Yablans' suite at Paramount with Howard Minsky, the now-famous producer who'd asked Charley to round up film extras in 1969. Since it had been Yablans' successful marketing of *Love Story* that propelled the former Sales VP to the company's presidency, Charley assumed that Paramount had become Minsky's oyster. He was shocked to hear that Minsky was in a state of anxiety because he couldn't get a green-light on his next project, even as Yablans was still holding out on money that Paramount owed him for *Love Story*.

"A light bulb went off over my head," Charley remembers. "I had one success with *Jessica*, and then a few failures. I was close to thirty. And Howard was close to sixty, an established producer with a good reputation. And here he was, with me, waiting to see this arrogant Paramount asshole, begging for the money he was owed. Right there in that moment, I said to myself, 'I'm not doing this anymore. I don't want to be doing this in thirty years when I'm sixty.'"

Minsky, the man who had brought Charley into the business, and inadvertently led him out. Soon after returning to New York, Charley joined the family business full time and launched himself into a new multiplex development in Yonkers. Glamour-wise, it was a comedown from film production. But at least this meant that the next time he'd be meeting with Paramount—or any studio—he'd be on the buy side.

Charley also was able to fold up his producer's chair knowing that he actually got the better of Paramount and the veteran Yablans on that one profitable film he made. The typical deal structure, at the time, had the distributor (in this case, Paramount) taking a percentage of the film's gross box-office earnings as a "distribution fee," typically 25 percent, plus all the expenses associated with marketing and creating physical prints. The producer would get whatever was left after the exhibitors took their cut, which generally ranged from nothing to not much. Charley intuited immediately what many producers learned the hard way: that any accounting system that left the studios in charge of tallying up their expenses had a built-in incentive for abuse. So Charley instead offered Yablans a full 70 percent off the gross, with the proviso that Paramount would fund all of their expenses out of that 70 percent share (what became known as a "gross deal").

Crucially, the deal specified that the TV revenues would be flipped, with Charley and the other producers getting 75 percent of television licensing revenues, and Paramount getting 25 percent. Since no one at Paramount thought that terrifying fare like *Jessica* would ever be shown on television (the movie actually received an X rating in the UK), Yablans believed he was giving Charley 75 percent of nothing. But in 1976, just as *Diary of the Dead* was bombing at theaters, *Jessica* was freaking out millions of Americans in their living rooms: in a move that would have seemed unimaginable just a few years earlier, ABC had made this ghoulish tale of madness and murder its Movie of the Week.

While the five years that Charley spent as a film producer taught him a lot about the business, and even allowed him to turn a small profit, that's not what he values most about that period of his professional life. "When you watch people at the Oscars giving those speeches about how everyone on the film became like a family, that's not just talk," he told me. "While you see a whole bunch of people on the credits for our films, there were really only like ten or twelve key people at the center of things. We would stay at the same hotels. We would have meals together. You shared all the emotions—and passions—that went with the ups and down of making the film. It's a gypsy kind of relationship, because these 'families' dissolve after the movie gets made. But for as long as it lasted, it truly was as much fun as I've ever had in my life."

Like his grandfather and father before him, Charley Moss had stepped just far enough into the world of content creation to glimpse the glamorous but shallow and often soul-destroying culture of Hollywood, and to know that he preferred the business of film exhibition. It would provide more than enough challenges to keep him occupied in the decades ahead.

CHAPTER TEN

The Bertelsmann Imbroglio

TIMES SQUARE'S REPUTATION WAS as low as ever when Charles B. Moss died, and its future as a film exhibition hub looked bleak. While the paparazzi and celebrities might still come out for a big opening night, ordinary filmgoers were wary. It wasn't just that the area had become an ugly sludge of porn shops and tourist traps. It had actually become dangerous.

The hollowing out of Manhattan's unionized manufacturing industries in the postwar decades destroyed the city's middle class, exacerbated racial tensions, and convinced more than a million New Yorkers to follow the Mosses out to the suburbs. Gangs took over whole neighborhoods (especially in the Bronx, which became a byword for misery), enriching themselves through the sale of heroin. The Son-of-Sam murderer David Berkowitz was a fresh memory in everyone's mind.

The city's infrastructure sometimes seemed on the verge of complete collapse. A massive power outage had put New York on the cover of *Time* magazine—a picture of chaos under the headline "Blackout '77—Once More With Looting." Some of the movies being shown at Moss's own theaters, such as *Escape From New York*, depicted the city as one big hellhole.

And the city's unions, embittered by layoffs, distributed a leaflet to tourists entitled *Welcome to Fear City: A Survival Guide for Visitors.* Among its recommendations: stay indoors after 6 p.m.

At the 1920 dedication of the Coliseum, one of his most famous film houses, B.S. Moss had compared New York to ancient Rome in the glory days of Vespasian. When Charley looked out onto Broadway in the late 1970s, he felt more like Nero. Having been instrumental in his father's decision to hang on to the Criterion, he now had to make it work in an entertainment environment that refused to sit still.

The ascension of Charley to a position of leadership in the family business also coincided with a profound shift in the artistic conventions within film—one reflected by his own modest oeuvre. The celebrity-driven film world that marked Charles Sr.'s heyday had been a top-down monoculture dictated from on high by studio and network chiefs. But the counter-culturalists among Charley's generation of college grads found this climate suffocating. "What paid studio bills in the mid-1960s were James Bond extravaganzas, John Wayne westerns, Elvis Presley quickies, Dean Martin action comedies, and a long-standing willingness on the part of moviegoers to suspend disbelief," *Entertainment Weekly* editor Mark Harris wrote in his 2008 book *Pictures At A Revolution.* "Now, suddenly, people also wanted *Blow-Up* and *The Dirty Dozen* and Clint Eastwood's *Man With No Name* and Bob Dylan in *Don't Look Back.*"

This transition meant that the range of available content was expanding, and that audiences were not only fleeing the cities but fragmenting. The idea of a single mass audience was dying. There were still blockbusters such as *Star Wars* and *Indiana Jones and the Temple of Doom*, but independent cinema was coming on strong. These trends undermined a core presumption that had been embedded within the Moss family's business model since early days: that its circuit should be anchored by a prestigious first-run, single-screen cinema in Manhattan, the heart of American arts and culture.

Glamorous premieres were becoming a thing of the past. Few people were going to make the trip in from the suburbs just to see a movie. Not when America's suburbs were simultaneously sprouting multiplexes in malls and on commercial strips. These new venues might be concrete islands of film functionality amidst seas of asphalt, but they offered real choice, a movie for every taste. With studios now reluctant to give long-running exclusives to a particular movie palace, the multiplexes were more than competitive.

The grandiose single-screen theaters built by B.S. Moss and his generation were meant to serve densely populated urban centers. One by one, starting in the late 1970s, they began to close. They were torn down or converted to other uses. (It was a slow process. The former Moss & Brill's Hamilton Theatre on Broadway at 146th Street, as of this writing, has been languishing on the market at a sale price of $8 million. During his last tour of the place, says Charley, he was confronted with rat nests and skeletons of dead cats.)

As the movie-viewing experience changed, so did the role of the theater owner. In the early and middle decades of the twentieth century, B.S. Moss and his son Charles both were required, by industry convention, to trade on their public image to promote their theaters. But as blockbuster premieres became less common, and film became just one form of mass-media entertainment among many, the role of an exhibitor became similar to that of any other business executive. Even the largest American theater circuits—AMC, Regal, Cinemark—now are led by executives who are as unknown to ordinary Americans as the men and women who run insurance companies and banks. Not that Charley Moss lamented the shift. Like his father, he preferred to keep a low media profile.

Charley's biggest challenge initially was to make a go of the Criterion theater and its building, which he now owned entirely. Jerome Greene had been bought out of his 25 percent share. On Charles B. Moss's death, Greene had tried to bully Charley into selling the Bow Tie asset. He said the Canadian developer Robert Campeau was offering to pay double what the Mosses had paid for the building. Rather than sell, Charley took a larger mortgage and waved Greene off. Greene responded by suing the Moss family, unsuccessfully, on the conflict-of-interest claims he'd once explicitly waived.

The Criterion Theatre was now divided up into multiple screens and Charley was facing challenges in maintaining traditional quality standards.

In one notorious 1982 incident, reported in great detail by a *New York Times* reporter in attendance, the Criterion's premiere 70mm showing of *Blade Runner* glitched badly, and had to be cut short before the movie was finished.

A few weeks later, when another *Times* reporter was invited to do a more detailed story on the multiplex's back office, she found a confined workplace that, as in theaters all across North America during this strained period, was oriented toward controlling costs instead of improving customer experience:

> At the Criterion, the same projectionist is in charge of both upstairs theaters, which are several flights of stairs apart. A warning system in each projection booth indicates whether the film in the other booth is still running. But the warning system doesn't indicate anything more, whether the film is in focus, whether the sound is right, whether there are problems in the audience. Down in the basement, the projectionist is even busier, running four theaters out of two cramped projection rooms. The theaters are so close together that it's possible, if a film is a big enough hit, to run it simultaneously on two different screens by stringing it through two different projectors and across the length of a projection booth, almost as if it were clothesline. Charles Moss, head of the B.S. Moss Organization, which owns the Criterion, makes no great arguments for this arrangement. "I knew those theaters weren't going to be knockouts when we built them," he explained. "But they give us a chance to show films in Midtown that the public wouldn't otherwise be able to see. Nowadays, if a film takes in $10,000 or $15,000 in a midtown theater, that's not enough to maintain it in a larger house, and so the film closes. We can keep something longer because our operating costs are low."

Finding and keep tenants in the Criterion building was equally challenging. It was a renters' market, and Charley often wound up working with characters more colorful than he would have preferred. A pair of cousins (related to each other, not to Charley) leased the second-floor space that formerly had been the flagship Bond clothing shop. They converted the space into a disco and were too cheap to change the sign. They simply called it Bond's and gave it a *Moonraker* theme in honor of Agent 007. (A press report noted that "the last guys who tried to build a disco [in the building] were going to call it The Pharaoh, with an Egyptian décor. Seems nobody was eager to put money into an Arabian-type disco. Not during the oil shortage.")

Another thing the cousins did was play fast and loose with the government. One day in 1982, Charley showed up at the Bow Tie Building to find the whole place padlocked and plastered with signs reading "Closed by order of the Treasury Department." It turned out that his tenants had been operating several sets of books. Both men ended up in jail but, amazingly, succeeded in keeping their liquor license (felons aren't allowed to hold liquor licenses in New York). The nightclub was closed during the eighteen months its owners spent in jail, but they kept paying their rent. They were eager to resume business on their release and kept phoning Charley from prison to ensure he didn't rent the space to someone else. These calls were made on a collect basis. Memories of phone operators asking Charley's children, Ben and Elizabeth, and their mother, Robin, if they would accept a call from Allenwood Federal Penitentiary remain firmly entrenched in Moss lore. Although they were in breach of their lease from any number of directions, Charley let them keep the space. It was not as though he had a line-up of alternative tenants.

While Charley lost $750 thousand on the building in the first year things quickly stabilized. Sketchy as the disco project was on the ownership side, it was a huge hit with customers. When it was set to open, a reporter gushed that "the place will hold 5,000 disco dancers," and perhaps even draw so many "celebs" as to "cripple Studio 54."

In the course of digging out of his financial hole, Charley decided it was time to confront his unions. He had no problem with his staff being unionized, but the expectations of some of the guilds were patently ridiculous. The union representing stage hands, for instance, required Charley to employ two stagehands at each theater, never mind that they showed no live performances and had no need of a single stagehand. It was classic union featherbedding. Charley couldn't fire the stage hands: their union would have put up a picket line, and the projectionists would have refused to cross it, leaving the theater dark. So he kept employing the stagehands, who would come in weekly to pick up their cheques and never be seen again, until, finally, Charley was fed up. "I thought it was finally time to take a stand," he says. "I hate getting ripped off. I don't mind spending money, but it really bothers me to get ripped off."

Charley convinced his fellow theater owners that it was worthwhile trying to get rid of the useless stage hands. They agreed. Inevitably, all the theaters were hit with a strike. It was left to Charley to negotiate with the union's representative, Bob MacDonald. "We called each other names and the rest of it," says Charley, "but after dinner and a couple of glasses of wine, we were able to come to terms, and we formed a good relationship. Bob became to me the same sort of ally that Steve D'Inzillo was to my father."

During the 1980s, Charley's fortunes had improved sufficiently that he managed to stage an ambitious transformation of the Bow Tie building, developing it into a mixed-use entertainment space called The Criterion Center. To get it done, he needed Bob MacDonald's help.

Crucial to the Criterion Center plan was installing a live Broadway theater in place of the Bond nightclub. Charley's vision was to give live-show producers the opportunity to produce award-winning plays and musicals in a venue without the usual union overhead. Only shows performed in the geographically defined Broadway theater district are eligible to be nominated for Tony Awards. The Bow Tie building was within those borders, so that hurdle was cleared. Getting a break from the unions was the bigger challenge. They were all over Broadway, so much so that every theater had to employ one person whose only job was to sweep the stage before the show began. Charley decided to offer Bob MacDonald a deal.

"One of the things about Broadway theaters is that when they don't have a show, they go dark," says Charley. "My pitch to Bob was that we'd guarantee employment for the one stagehand we needed, 52-weeks a year, but we wanted no more employees than we genuinely needed. It would keep our costs lower. For the union, the trade-off was fewer jobs but more job security. And that was the deal we made."

The more Charley thought about the Criterion Center project, the more ambitious he became for it. He expanded the concept to include a restaurant, bar, and cabaret space in addition to the 600-seat live theater. The venues were built. Professionals were hired to run various new pieces. They opened, and almost immediately ran into financial trouble. Still, not enough people were venturing out to Times Square for an evening's entertainment.

The one good thing that came out of Bow Tie's new troubles was that the live theater community heard about them. The principals at the Roundabout, an off-Broadway (and Tony ineligible) theater company, saw an opportunity for them to move into the Broadway loop. They offered to rent the live theater from Charley. He agreed. The Roundabout moved in and operated out of the space for more than a decade, taking some of the heat from Bow Tie.

It wasn't until the 1990s, more than a decade after he had first staked the future of his family's business on the rebirth of Times Square, that it became obvious the Mosses had made the right decision. By then, the city was rein-venting the Deuce, and Disney was renovating the New Amsterdam Theatre as a venue for *The Lion King*. Violent crime, which had peaked citywide in 1990 and 1991, now was plummeting under the proactive police methods championed by Mayor Rudy Giuliani.

In 1998, Charley got a chance to cash out in a big way. Bertelsmann, the German multinational corporation that had long ago acquired the sky-scraper on the other side of Forty-Fifth Street (site of the former Loew's State Theatre, as noted earlier), was looking to expand. Its offer to Charley was $92 million for the rights to erect an office building in the airspace above the Moss's retail space and Criterion Theatre. The tower would accommo-date Bertelsmann's newly acquired Random House assets, which would be connected to the existing Bertelsmann Building via a neon-lit sky bridge.

As the business press saw it, this was a no-brainer for Charley, who'd be able to make almost twenty times his family's original investment on the real estate (and more than 200 times its original cash layout) while keeping his own building and continuing on with the family tradition of film exhibition as lessor. But Charley balked at Bertelsmann's offer.

The crucial part of the deal involved the extent to which the thick col-umns necessary to support the planned skyscraper would break up Charley's ground-level retail and theater space. "The value of our building is in its location at the heart of Times Square," says Charley, "but also in the fact that it has 30,000-square-feet of space with thirty-foot ceilings and no pillars. To some users, like theaters, that's invaluable." He negotiated hard with Bertelsmann to ensure that the columns would not affect his own space, or at least that they would disrupt the least valuable space. They came to an agreement but Bertelsmann reneged at the eleventh-hour, claiming that the lack of columns was driving up the cost of the skyscraper. It wanted to double, roughly, the number of columns. Charley was expected to acquiesce. He didn't.

He told Bertelsmann that the new columns, which would disrupt his prime real estate space, were a deal-breaker. That led to a meeting with Bertelsmann's chief executive who made a few arrogant comments and raised his offer to $100 million. "To be perfectly honesty with you," Charley told him, "I don't trust this anymore." He walked. He preferred to keep the sense of control that came with ownership. Besides, as he told his son Ben at the time, "If this is the honeymoon, imagine the marriage."

The failure of the deal brought Charley abuse from the press, particularly the *New York Times*. A real estate writer named Charles Bagli portrayed him as a rank amateur, claiming no serious businessman would have turned down such an opportunity (in a stunning coincidence, Jerome Greene's obituary ran on the reverse side of the page from Bagli's article). But Charley was convinced his property would be more valuable without an office building on top of it. Times Square, after all, is one of only a few high-density places in the entire developed urban world where owners enjoy the unrestricted right to put up rooftop commercial signage. He figured that with the influx of millions of tourists into the newly "Disneyfied" area, sign-leasing rates were set to skyrocket in coming years. In fact, they did.

It was in mid-1999, a few months after walking away from the Bertelsmann deal, and two decades after buying the Bow Tie Building, that Charley finally seems to have definitively won the respect of the Midtown real estate community. "We had clients like Jockey and Liz Claiborne leasing our signs," says Charley. "It was standard in the industry at the time for rents to be month-to-month. We went to our clients with an offer. We suggested they lock up the signs for the long term and enjoy the security that came with that. Normally, you'd get a discount leasing something for the long term, but we convinced them to pay a premium for the security."

The time, the press corps loved the deal: "Billboard deals bolster developer: Times Sq. site yields $50 mil. for owner who refused to build Bertelsmann tower," read one headline. The article underneath described how Charley had clinched sign-licensing deals worth a staggering $50 million for three billboard locations, with more deals on the way, on top of the $12 million being generated annually by retail tenants. (The numbers were exaggerated, but not by a lot.) "This validates the strategy we chose," declared Charley, who was by now a middle-aged veteran of the New York real estate wars.

There would be still more signage adventures for Charley. Part of his building wraps around 44th Street and has signs on the roof. Across the street, ABC leased second-floor space for a goldfish-bowl studio from which *Good Morning America* would be broadcast. The idea was to have Times Square as the background to the show. As it turned out, that put Bow Tie's building and signage right in the center of *Good Morning America's* frame. Charley did the sensible thing and walked across to ABC to suggest that if the network was going to broadcast the Bow Tie building three hours a day, it might want to buy the billboard on top to ensure NBC or CBS didn't put their logos on it. They came to terms, not without a lot of back-and-forth with ABC's bureaucracy.

Three or four months later, Charley landed Toys "R" Us as the street-level tenant on the 44th Street Corner. It was a huge win for Bow Tie to have an established retail client open a flagship megastore in the space. The only problem was that Toys "R" Us was demanding access to the billboard on the roof. After coaxing ABC to buy that very billboard, Charley now had to return to the network and request a buyout after only a few months. Fortunately, ABC was owned by Disney, which sold a high-volume of goods at Toys "R" Us and a reasonable settlement was arranged.

Toys "R" Us had been a hard decision for Charley. Flagship tenant or not, it meant closing the Criterion and turning over its space to the retailer. All things considered, B.S. Moss would have understood the decision. With name-brand retailers clamoring to create a splashy Times Square presence, the space had become too valuable to dedicate to film exhibition, especially with AMC set to flood the market in 2000 with its 25-screen, 4,916 seat Empire 25 on Forty-Second Street, across the street from Regal's 20-screen counterpart. In addition to Toys "R" Us, the Bow Tie building leased to Old Navy, The Gap, Swatch, and Walgreens. Before long, the building was spinning cash. Charley and his family remain proud of their connection to Times Square. But there was never any sense in letting that feeling lapse into sentimentality.

* * *

In a small town, residents mourn the closing of a movie theater because it might be one of the few centers of civic life, and because the move usually symbolizes a broader economic malaise in the community. But the closing of the Criterion had the opposite significance: it closed because a hot local economy had boosted land valuations to such a point that the opportunity cost of film exhibition was too high. And in the 2000s, the area would become hotter than ever, even if the locus of consumer activity was shifting away from mass entertainment to high-end retail.

Charley and his son Ben did not take the sale of the Criterion as an opportunity to abandon film exhibition more generally. In fact, much of the revenue that would flow from the property would be re-invested in movie houses, new and old, in smaller, more affordable real estate markets that had been abandoned by other film exhibitors. Unlike other circuits, Bow Tie didn't have to take on a large debt load to finance its acquisitions and upgrades, thanks to its cash cow in Times Square.

CHAPTER ELEVEN

Investing in Zombie Land

NEIGHBORHOODS CHANGE, YEAR BY YEAR, decade by decade, and seldom in a straight line. B.S. Moss's Coliseum was built at 181st Street in Washington Heights when it was still a partly rural area. The theater flourished along with its local community until both living habits and movie-going changed. B.S. Moss sold the theater to RKO, and several other companies have run it since. In the nineties, it was carved up into retail space, with a quadplex theater built out of its former balcony. The Coliseum closed for good in 2011. At last glance, its building was boarded up, and its marquee advertised the last movies that ran: *Real Steel*, a robot boxing movie, and the medical thriller *Contagion*. A long-defunct second-floor business features a faded 1980s-era window advertisement for "BEEPERS: Easy Connection." The place looks like a tomb for film exhibition's golden age. Similar sites can be found up and down Broadway.

Northern Manhattan is now a bleak landscape for commercial movie exhibition: since the shuttering of the AMC Magic in Harlem in 2019, there is not a single screen to be found. But it would be foolish to bet against a motion-picture comeback of some variety. Things once looked equally unpromising in some of the smaller cities where Charley and Ben Moss have managed to build thriving movie houses in recent years. While the film industry traditionally has been about bringing big-city glamour to middle America, the task of revitalizing old husks such as the Coliseum in Manhattan, along with the civic culture they anchored, may now require Gotham to take lessons from its smaller urban cousins.

New Haven, Connecticut was an industrial powerhouse in the 1930s, producing everything from clocks to guns. One of its most impressive companies was United Illuminating Co, which erected its landmark head-quarters at 80 Temple Street. In classic Colonial Revival style, the office building featured an elegant-four-sided clock tower, ground-floor walls pan-eled in polished marble, and interior lobby with large murals depicting the history of electric power.

When UI moved out in 1992, the building fell on hard times, much like rusted-out New Haven, a hundred miles northwest of Manhattan along the north shore of Long Island Sound. First one developer, then another, tried and failed to find a profitable way to adapt the building to modern use. Throughout the 1990s, it sat empty, gathering dust and graffiti, amidst an inner-city no-man's-land of bars, parking garages, and other unused properties. Those were the sights awaiting Charley and Ben Moss when a real-estate broker showed them the building in 2003.

By this time, the Charley Moss had become concerned that the fam-ily business was becoming too one-dimensional: the Bow Tie Building in New York was generating as much revenue as all its suburban theaters put together. It was a lot of value to be tied up in a single block of real estate, and so Charley and Ben looked to invest profits in the undervalued core areas of smaller cities. With its large tech sector, teaching hospital, and world-class university (Yale), New Haven seemed as good a bet as any.

The original Moss plan in New Haven wasn't complicated: buy the build-ing, preserve the stately shell, gut the innards, and create high-end apartments for young couples and empty nesters. As Charley and Ben saw things, the development could be the first stirrings of a gradual transformation that moved Bow Tie Cinemas' core business from movie theaters to real estate. But what they saw when they toured 80 Temple Street changed their minds.

When UI opened the headquarters building in 1940, the company built it as a hub for every single part of its commercial operations, from the president's office to the call center. At the front of the building, under the clock-tower rotunda, were a series of tellers whom local customers could call on to pay bills, change their service plans, and buy UI-branded electric gadgets such as washing machines, ranges, water heaters, and refrigerators. Off to the left were the accounting and billing departments. Off to the right were the executive suites. On the south side were two large truck bays, which opened onto a seventy-vehicle service garage in the basement. In a typical apartment building, the ceilings might provide as little as seven-or-eight feet clearance. But UI's basement had ceilings at least three times that height, an architectural necessity, since that was where the company's emergency-services vehicles and meter-installation vans were stored and serviced. UI was essentially running a medium-sized trucking company out of an office-building basement.

Charley still remembers the day he and Ben first toured that underground area. At the time, their minds were focused on maximizing the number of apartments they could fit into the building envelope. From that perspective, soaring ceilings presented a challenge: there was no inexpensive way to convert efficiently all that vertical space to residential or retail use. Perhaps they could turn it into an auditorium space, Charley thought. Or a gym, or . . .

Neither Charley nor Ben remembers who said it, but they agree that one of them did: "Hey, you know what? We could probably fit a movie theater in here."

Two years later, in November 2004, Charley and Ben opened New Haven's Criterion Cinemas within a 44-unit apartment complex that they called Temple Square. Two years after that, with business booming, they added two more screens. As of this writing, there are nine.

The project became part of a larger renaissance in the area. "Until a few years ago, Temple Street and the surrounding area . . . were a depressed and unattractive part of downtown," the *New York Times* reported in 2004. "As part of a city rehabilitation program, [the area has] become an increasingly lively locus of new boutiques, nightclubs and restaurants."

In the fifteen years since that project opened, Charley and Ben have launched other downtown building and restoration projects in many cities. As in New Haven, they often faced considerable skepticism but, in general, they've proven critics wrong. The biggest circuits take a cookie-cutter approach to building theaters—which appear in malls as freshly constructed, purpose-built concrete boxes. The idea of carving a theater out of a downtown heritage building simply doesn't fall into their business plan. As with the rise of craft beer and artisanal coffee products, it's an example of a smaller, more innovative supplier developing a growing niche market that can't be served by legacy players invested in established forms of mass consumption.

These restoration projects also spurred intergenerational renewal within the Moss family business. Just as Charley Moss had helped convince his father to hang on to the Criterion when Times Square was tarnished by crime and squalor in the 1970s, Ben was spurring a middle-aged Charley to rejuvenate the family's theater circuit after years of contraction.

* * *

Every important American city once had its own smaller version of Times Square and, in the case of Richmond, Virginia, it was the downtown area that now encompasses the neighborhoods known as Jackson Ward and Court End. Jackson Ward was once was celebrated as "the Harlem of the South," and even had its own version of the Deuce (the Second Street strip that ran through the heart of the district). The latter area, Court End, became home to countless upscale outlets including the Richmond Theatre, whose 1811 destruction by fire was, at the time, the deadliest urban disaster in American history. Seventy-two victims perished, including the governor of Virginia. And many more might have died, if not for the bravery of a blacksmith slave named Gilbert Hunt who helped many to escape. While a few of Richmond's old theaters remain as live performance venues, the vast majority have been torn down in favor of office buildings, retail space, and government offices.

Richmond's population is just 230,000, yet few cities can rival its rich connection to American history. Two blocks north of the former Richmond

Theatre sits the White House of the Confederacy, the executive residence of Confederate president Jefferson Davis. Two blocks west of that is John Marshall House, former home of one of America's greatest jurists. A stone's throw from that is the home of Maggie L. Walker, a black-rights activist who was the first female bank president in U.S. history. Continue westward, and you can walk along Monument Avenue, which featured statues of J. E. B. Stuart, Robert E. Lee, and Stonewall Jackson, at least until the civil unrest of 2020. The Monument Avenue Historic District formally ends at Roseneath Road, where visitors are greeted with a statue honoring a very different figure: Richmond-born black tennis legend Arthur Ashe (1943–93). Appearing at the end of a strip that has celebrated nineteenth-century Confederate generals, the 1996 statue serves as a sort of 12-foot-high bronze historical punctuation mark, symbolically setting off the present from the Confederate ghosts memorialized elsewhere on the boulevard.

Follow Broad Street west out of downtown, through Jackson Ward and the nominal "Arts District," and you'll find black neighborhoods full of shuttered storefronts and urban blight. Racial inequality is a daily reality in Richmond, embedded in the city's geography. While the historical heart of the city is occupied by wealthy whites, much of its black periphery remains impoverished and neglected.

Keep walking west toward the Science Museum, though, and the scenery does eventually yield signs of hope. Many of the bones of old Richmond remain, but they've been put to new uses—as with the Interbake Foods building, an iconic 1927 cookie factory that recently was turned into a 178-unit apartment building. Turn right on Arthur Ashe Boulevard, and you'll find yourself situated amidst the signs of a germinating hipster colony: an upscale taco restaurant (El Su Boca), a tattoo parlor (River City), a coffee "roast lab" (Lamplighter), a world-class barbecue restaurant (ZZQ), not one but two cideries (Buskey and Blue Bee), and Bow Tie Cinemas' twenty-one-screen Movieland multiplex, opened in 2009 as the first new movie theater the city had seen since an art house cinema called the Biograph opened in 1972 (and closed fifteen years later).

When the Mosses created their Movieland Richmond facility, the area they picked, Scott's Addition, was somewhat analogous to the depressed

New Haven neighborhood they'd chosen for Bow Tie Criterion Cinemas five years earlier. As the name implies, the neighborhood was tacked on to the city as an afterthought by one General Winfield Scott, and for decades remained an obscure jumble of warehouses, factories and strip joints. Local historian Harry Kollatz Jr. described it as "a cheap and gritty place accommodating lingering light industry and starving artists." One local described it to Kollatz as a "zombie land." A sign of the then-depressed state of the local economy is that, when the cinema opened in 2009, the Mosses got 3,200 applications for the fifty jobs on offer. At the same time, more than four thousand people applied early for the cinema's customer-loyalty program, a sign of pent-up demand.

Even at the time, before the neighborhood's current renaissance had begun, Charley and Ben Moss remember seeing potential in the property that eventually became Movieland, a nineteenth-century vintage factory then being used by a metal-forming company called Richmond Steel. The owner was a well-known local entrepreneur named Tommy Mayers, who at the time was entertaining offers from various buyers. "On the day we said yes to the deal, he took us out to lunch at a local place, and when it was time to head back to his office—this is something I still remember—he asked the waitress to pack up his white bread and mashed potatoes," Charley told me. "He came off as an aw-shucks kind of guy. But there was also something odd about this. We knew he was a sophisticated and successful operator. This was a guy who had four or five high-end motorboats—so maybe this was part of an act to put us off guard, but we weren't sure."

New York City has a certain reputation, and so the Mosses are careful to avoid any hint of arrogance when they negotiate deals in other parts of the country. Yet Charley tells me that he also has to be careful of locals playing on small-market rube stereotypes as a means to get the Mosses' guard down during negotiations. To this day, in fact, he isn't sure if Tommy Mayers really had any intention of eating those leftovers, or if it was just part of his "aw-shucks" act.

"Ben and I had told Tommy that we needed to renegotiate the price we'd be paying under our arrangement," Charley remembers. "We told him we'd have to pay him less because we'd discovered unanticipated development costs. Tommy doesn't say yes or no—but he does remind us of those other interested buyers he'd originally been speaking to. He invites us back to his plant after lunch and sits us down in his office. Then, right in front of us, he picks up the phone, dials a number, and says into the phone, 'Hey, remember that property you wanted? Well, turns out it's still available. Let's set up a meeting.' Then he listens for a bit, hangs up and dials another number and does the same thing. Then he hung up and did it again. By this time, Ben and I are laughing. Mayers' performance is worthy of an Academy Award. Finally we just tell him we'll pay him the full price we'd agreed to originally. Every dollar. Tommy got his money. And when we opened Movieland a few years later, he was there having a wonderful time, and very proud of what we'd done with his property. But to this day, I have no idea whether there was anyone on the other end of those phone calls."

* * *

There's no magic formula for rehabilitating a neighborhood. Scott's Addition does provide a case study in regard to some of the key ingredients, however: attractive public-transit options; a local college population (in this case, Virginia Commonwealth University); low rents; and a critical mass of millennial entrepreneurs, tech start-ups, artisans, and other assorted "makers" whose flexible business models allow them to work out of repurposed industrial spaces. Yet, if these areas are to blossom into middle-class communities that young couples don't abandon as soon as their first child arrives, they also need to attract old-fashioned retail amenities such as supermarkets, day-cares, restaurants and, yes, movie theaters.

To this day, Richmond's neighborhoods still bear the imprint of a 1911 ordinance designating where blacks and whites could live. That system of de jure segregation was struck down by the courts, but the racist intent was preserved in race-based covenants stipulated in property deeds that weren't invalidated until 1948. Scott's Addition, at 63 percent white and 30 percent black, is less segregated than many other parts of Richmond. And Movieland draws its audience from a variety of local neighborhoods, including the poorer, blacker areas that lie to the east, and the wealthier, whiter areas that lie to the north and south. In this era, it shouldn't count as unusual for a business to feature a racially diverse clientele mixing casually on an everyday basis. Unfortunately, in some parts of the United States, it does. When the Mosses were first embarking on the $9-million Movieland project in the late 2000s, they received veiled warnings from locals to the effect that the area's mixed demography might present "challenges." They ignored these warnings, and the theater is now a profitable business, widely hailed by locals as a key factor in the rise of Scott's Addition over the last decade.

Having learned hard lessons about how new construction projects can destroy neighborhoods, the city of Richmond and the state of Virginia, like other American jurisdictions, now take a more enlightened approach to local development. This includes the provision of tax breaks for companies, like Bow Tie, that protect neighborhoods' historic architectural character. Movieland's first seventeen screens were built in a complex that had operated between 1887 and 1927 as the Richmond Locomotive Works assembly plant, with a small brass foundry being subsequently turned into a four-screen art-house cinema. During construction, the Mosses made a virtue of necessity by commissioning an attractive architectural design that showcases the steel-and-brick sinew of the original building. Near the front entrance, columns and girders from the Locomotive Works soar out of the ground, creating a public-art tribute to the structure's nineteenth-century origins. The main lobby is decorated with two large paintings of the Richmond Tramp and Southern 1401 locomotives, two famed models once produced on site. Ironically, the Mosses have found that one way to build the best "theater of tomorrow" is to pay proper homage to the past. It also didn't hurt that this Movieland complex also happened to be the first cinema in the state of Virginia licensed to serve alcohol.

* * *

One last note about Richmond, Virginia. If B.S. Moss had a local equivalent, it might have been Jake Wells, a former baseball player who built the Bijou vaudeville theater on Broad Street in 1899, and once was christened the "father of Richmond movie houses." According to a chronology assembled by a member of the Richmond-based James River Film Society, "with his brother Otto, Jake expanded into the Norfolk market, opening the Granby. In the early 1920s, the mighty Wells chain included forty-two theaters in the Southeast." But then Wells' story takes a tragic turn: in 1927, he "drove out to the countryside, shot himself in the head—twice!—and died."

CHAPTER TWELVE

Hellboys and Tentpoles

THERE ARE ALMOST 150,000 hotel rooms in Las Vegas but for film buffs, the *Rain Man* suite on the sixty-sixth floor of Caesars Palace stands out. It is the Oscar-sanctified spot where Tom Cruise's Charlie Babbitt taught Dustin Hoffman's Raymond how to dance and made the mistake of trying to hug him. The 2019 CinemaCon, a Las Vegas trade show for film exhibitors, was held at Caesars Palace and the two-floor *Rain Man* suite (which books for about four thousand dollars a night) was functioning as the hospitality venue for WebMedia, a company that provides film exhibitors and other clients with web platforms and phone apps.

Bow Tie Cinemas, the film circuit now run by Charley Moss Jr. and his son Ben, is a WebMedia client, and together with their chief operating officer, Joseph Masher, they made the obligatory appearance at the hospitality suite. WebMedia's products help Bow Tie's film-going customers find show-time information and purchase tickets in advance. They also allow Bow Tie's managers to send out individualized offers and newsletters to regulars based on viewing habits and geolocation. At the suite, the Moss entourage heard Malcolm MacMillan, Webmedia's executive vice-president for global exhibitor relations, rattle off a list of numbers harvested from WebMedia's software over the last year. The Bow Tie website's "conversion rate," the percentage of customers who bought movie tickets after arriving at the company's web page, sat at 3.43 percent, on track with the industry standard of 3.5 percent for general-admission theaters. Just over 80 percent of visitors were being directed to the site from online search engines: a significantly higher number than the industry average of 69 percent.

This trove of data, and discussions of phone apps and web platforms, is now integral to the operations of a modern motion-picture circuit. It would have been Greek to B.S. Moss, but at bottom the major questions are unchanged since his time. Who's coming to the movies? How much are they spending? How can we make sure they come back?

In B.S. Moss' era, the challenge was to convince upscale consumers that a premium movie house was a perfectly respectable place for a middle-class person to spend an evening or afternoon. Today, Charley and Ben Moss have to find ways to attract customers to movie theaters within an entertainment landscape that allows people to watch movies on TVs, tablets, and phones. In both eras, the men who've led the Moss business found their solutions in architecture and the viewing experience. For B.S. Moss, it was the movie palace, that "more beautiful and sumptuous edifice" he would rhapsodize about to his fellow theater owners. For his grandson and great-grandson, it means the creation of VIP rooms, upscale hospitality options, fixtures such as reclining seats, and high-tech audiovisual technology installations.

After the WebMedia meeting wrapped up, the Bow Tie delegation attended a presentation by Jon Taffer, host of the popular TV show *Bar Rescue*, the plot of which typically involves Taffer inspecting some failing bar, shouting at the employees, and remaking the place in a commercially successful way. It might seem odd to have a bar-turnaround specialist speak at a convention aimed at cinema operators but one of the core messages Taffer delivered in his talk is that bar owners, restaurateurs, movie exhibitors, and pretty much everyone else in the retail entertainment sector, are in the same business: they're all trying to elicit a *reaction* from consumers in a way that draws them out of their homes.

"Everyone has a kitchen, but people still come out to eat," Taffer told the audience. "A cook may think he's producing an entrée, but I tell him that what he's trying to produce is a reaction. Take a look at the diner sitting in his chair. What you want is for him to sit up and get excited about that food when the waiter puts it in front of him. If that's not happening, why is he coming out to eat? Why not just eat at home?"

A century ago, it was class snobbery that kept people at home. In our own era, it's laziness and consumer choice. Modern customers can watch movies in a dozen different ways, and are bombarded by the other media, such as premium television series and even high-end narrative-driven video games, that have co-opted film techniques and film idioms to tell their stories. This pressure continues to drive innovation in the film-exhibition business. And it is notable that the period when film-exhibition quality was at its lowest ebb corresponds to the late Cold War period, which is when suburban theaters already had become a commodity retail business but before their owners faced competition from videotapes, DVDs. As in all spheres, the greatest enemy of product excellence is complacency.

Anyone walking the trade-show kiosks at CinemaCon would get a taste of what kind of innovation has been produced by modern competitive pressures. Admittedly, some of the commercial representatives were simply selling variations on old standards, such as the PepsiCo representatives pushing Cheetos Popcorn (regular popcorn garnished in Cheetos-scented oil and mixed in with Cheetos corn puffs), or the Tootsie Roll vendor boasting of a new format that eliminates the individual wrappers. "There's less crap for your guests to throw on the floor," the Tootsie Roll rep told one interested visitor. But there were also true technological marvels, including a lighting system produced by an LED manufacturer that can illuminate the interior of a small screening room at full luminescence with less than 150 watts of power (about as much as is used by two old-fashioned incandescent bulbs), and a wireless-equipment provider whose earpiece-based system allowed viewers to watch an English-language movie while listening to the audio track in any language of their choice. The latter innovation went hand-in-hand with panel discussions of the best ways to serve not only blacks but Latinos, Asians, and other distinct groups.[7]

---

7   No retail-entertainment business can flourish today without taking stock of America's chang-ing demographics, not to mention the exploding foreign market. In 2009, there were about 4,700 movie screens in China. In 2019, there are about 66,000, 50 percent more than the 41,000 in the United States, according to National Association of Theater Owners statistics.

Cinergy Entertainment Group was at CinemaCon showing off its electronic in-seat food-and-beverage ordering system. This embeds itself in the armrests of the modern premium seats now common in VIP theaters. The system is designed to operate at low luminescence and has four separate light filters to ensure that the display is visible only to a user whose eyes are situated immediately above the screen.

Dolby took over a main theater at the conference to display a stunning promotional video sequence for Dolby's Atmos and Vision systems, the latest industry standards for audio and video, respectively. These hammered home the point that there are some immersive cinematic experiences that really can't be had at home.

Of course, none of this would move the needle on theatrical attendance if studios don't make films that people wanted to see. And one of the functions of CinemaCon is to allow exhibitors to get a taste of coming attractions and provide studios with feedback about conditions in local markets. Over the years, this feedback mechanism has helped drive some of the most important cultural changes that have taken place in Hollywood, especially the production of movies that reflect the more diverse audiences that theater owners now cater to. While repeatedly boasting of the studios' collective record-breaking $12-billion domestic box office in 2018 ($40 billion internationally), CinemaCon speakers noted that some of the biggest action hits probably weren't movies that would have been made a generation ago, because they featured stars who weren't white or male, including, most notably, the megahit *Black Panther*.

Fittingly enough, the main venue where CinemaCon attendees watched all these speeches and movie trailers is called The Colosseum. Caesars Palace built it especially for Celine Dion in 2001. She has delivered over a thousand shows in this venue, grossing upwards of $650 million in the process. No matter what you think of Dion's crooning, the phenomenon she represents shows how difficult it is for new media to kill off old art forms. In the early twentieth century, many artists worried that the phonograph, movies, radio and then television would spell the end for live entertainment of precisely the type that Dion provides. Yet while vaudeville's been dead since the 1930s, live entertainment is bigger than ever. In fact, the Las Vegas strip itself is home to massively profitable acts that would be recognizable to any old-time vaudevillian: comedians, illusionists, animal acts, acrobats, dancers, impressionists, sometimes combined in the form of modern variety shows. Amidst the buskers and street-side acts, one can even find caricaturists, silhouette artists, and mimes.

Some entertainment technologies really do die away. No one listens to music on 8-track anymore, or watches movies on laserdiscs. But technology aside, the fundamental nature of movie exhibition is that of a social experience, albeit one whose quality can be affected enormously by technological, architectural, and aesthetic factors. This social aspect is the existential quality that originated in the first spark of genius exhibited by the Lumière brothers, when they realized that people would prefer to sit with their friends and watch a movie projected on a wall than stare downwards at the innards of one of Thomas Edison's arcade machines. There is little doubt that the iPhone presents a more formidable competitor to film exhibition than the kinetoscope. But it still seems a solid bet that the current generation of American film exhibitors won't be the last.

* * *

In April 2019, visitors arriving last minute to a particular downtown movie theater showing the new *Avengers* movie were out of luck. This was a modern theater, with all on-site ticket sales managed electronically. The only human working the front was a middle-aged manager whose job was to help customers use the ticket machines, and to inform them which movies were available and which were sold out. On this particular day, his job was essentially that of a public-address system, endlessly playing the same message: "*Avengers*? Sorry, that's sold out till Monday. No, I don't know of any other theaters which have tickets available . . . *Avengers*? Sorry, that's sold out till Monday . . ."

Of the theater's six screens, four were playing *Avengers: Endgame*, the latest instalment in a Marvel Studios franchise that launched in 2012. As things turned out, even this lopsided allocation of seats wasn't enough to meet demand. Everyone in the industry knew *Endgame* would bring in huge crowds. But with a record-setting worldwide opening-weekend box-office of $1.2 billion, *Endgame* turned out to be even more popular than expected. Although studios are good at predicting what kind of market they'll attract with their movies, it's still an inexact art.

Every film exhibitor tries its best to match supply to demand in each local market. At the heart of that effort is the weekly planning meeting, which, at the Times Square offices of Bow Tie Partners, as Charley and Ben Moss now call their company, takes place on Monday mornings. On Monday, April 8, 2019, eighteen days before *Endgame* hit the big screen, Ben, Bow Tie Cinemas chief operation officer Joseph Masher, vice-president of film and marketing Jared Milgram, and film and marketing assistant Alicia Vinci gathered in a windowless conference room in the Bow Tie Building. Joining them by teleconference from Denver was veteran film buyer Hank Lightstone, whose work with the Moss family extends back to the era of Charley B. Moss. In front of each were two sets of spreadsheets. The first listed the films playing on the 238 screens situated in Bow Tie's thirty-seven cinema locations, with data setting out how many guests saw each film over the weekend that had just ended. The second listed the proposed exhibition plan for the week to come (which, for film exhibitors, begins on a Friday and ends on a Thursday).

Even in early April, all the company's plans were being laid out with "A-Day" (April 26) very much in mind. It was the subject everyone was eager to talk about. Nevertheless, the meeting began in a business-as-usual way, with a rundown of the weekly totals, interspersed with industry scuttlebutt about any surprise hits (or flops), and loose predictions about the performance of films that would be opening in coming days.

"We're coming out of a $632,000 weekend with 0.44 percent market share overall," said Milgram, meaning that roughly 44 out of ever 1,000 moviegoers had been sitting in a Bow Tie cinema over the weekend. *Shazam!* brought in $216,000. "It over-performed, I think, and we had 0.42 percent of [that film's] $52-million [domestic] gross [box office]," continued Milgram. "It played young—a very young, accessible, kid-friendly movie." *Pet Sematary*, the horror remake of Stephen King's novel of the same name, was "pretty much on projection." And *Best of Enemies*, a civil-rights drama about the Ku Klux Klan that had grossed only $4.4 million in its opening weekend, "didn't do so strongly—it's a shame. Maybe we should give it another week to breathe." They decided to "split" *Best of Enemies* in some theaters, meaning that it would alternate on a screen with another movie, and "final it" (one last week) at others.

On the plus side, the room was upbeat about the April 12 opening of *Hellboy*, a superhero film reboot based on a comic character with a beyond-the-grave backstory. (As things turned out, the movie bombed after attracting scathing reviews. In the words of one critic: "Bereft of the imaginative flair that made earlier *Hellboy*s so enjoyable, this soulless reboot suggests Dante may have left a tenth circle out of his Inferno.") There also was some hope expressed for the offbeat animated film *Missing Link*. "[United Artists] really wants to get that thing out there," said Lightstone. "As long as we show it for a week, they're happy. They're not particularly concerned about holding us to weeks two or three. They just want to have a respectable opening."

Following this came a succinct chat about *After*, a poorly reviewed teen romantic drama. "Apparently, this series has a big digital e-reader following—kind of like a non-vampire version of *Twilight*, even more fangless," said Milgram. "It'll do well for the pre-tween audience," added Alicia. "*Five Feet Apart* [another youth-oriented romantic melodrama] did okay for us in a lot of theaters, so I guess if we have some room in the big multiplexes, we'll play it, but not in the quads and five-plexes."

"Then we've got *Breakthrough*," said Milgram. "It's a FOX faith-based film but with a wide release and a big cast, and should do well. Also, *Mary Magdalene* [starring Joaquin Phoenix as Jesus], an old [Harvey] Weinstein title, but we're not committed to it for more than a week, so we'll just play it where we have space."

Milgram finished with a brief discussion of the nineteenth-century historical drama *Peterloo*, and the Aretha Franklin concert film *Amazing Grace*. "That's going to be our strong art-house title for four-nineteen [April 19]— and maybe more than just art house. It did $19,000 per screen at openings in New York and L.A."

"There are a lot of *okay* titles here," said Milgram, summarizing the rundown as a whole, "but probably nothing with as much upside as *Shazam!*

and *Pet Sematary.* And nothing is jamming us up in a way that will prevent us from really going crazy with *Avengers.*"

One trend in the previous week's data was obvious: even when there was no true blockbuster on offer, the top-grossing movie typically was earning a third or more of each theater's overall revenues. At Bow Tie's sixteen-plex in Trumbull, CT, for instance, the weekend's total gross had been $74,189, $29,445 of which was generated by three screens dedicated to *Shazam!* This tally was roughly equivalent to the second, third, and fourth-best performing films combined; and roughly double the combined total gross of the eight poorest performing movies.

Numbers like these provide a snapshot explanation as to why film production companies and theater chains alike focus so closely on the big hits: consumer demand obeys an almost logarithmic pattern, with the most popular wide releases trumping the least popular by two or even three orders of magnitude.

There were 592 general-release movies in 2018, ranging from *Black Panther* ($700 million on four thousand screens) down to *Mobile Homes* ($449 on a single screen). Judging from publicly available domestic box office data, the year's top seventeen films (rounded out by *Crazy Rich Asians* at $174 million) generated box office earnings equivalent to the other 575 films put together. And these seventeen films generated an average of about 30 percent of their earnings in the first weekend of commercial release. *Avengers: Infinity War* had an opening weekend that out-earned the *entire* box-office gross of every other movie released in 2018 except *Black Panther, Incredibles 2, Jurassic Park: Fallen Kingdom, Deadpool 2,* and *Dr. Seuss' The Grinch.* It was in 1956 that Charles Moss declared, "only big hits could survive." It's as true now as it was then.

This is why, even a few weeks out from April 26, everyone in the windowless conference room at Bow Tie wasn't just thinking about the coming *Avengers* money storm, but *dreaming* about it. "A lot of exhibitors and third-party ticketers had issues with *Avengers* tickets going on sale last Tuesday," said Milgram. "But we did *not.* I woke up in a panic about it, and I wanted to see what the buzz was on Twitter. Number-one trend was '*Avengers: End Game* tickets,' and people were getting messages like, 'You're in line. It's going to be an hour to complete your purchase.' All the sites were buffering like that. And so I signed on to our own account to see what the comments were, and it was like 'Going to see *Avengers* at Bow Tie. Glad their website works.' There wasn't any problem on our end. I think we're up to $500,000 already [in pre-sales]."

By the time the meeting was over, the group had reviewed the film menu for every theater in the chain, one at a time, a granular and time-consuming process. According to Masher, this deliberative approach is something of a throwback. "Most other chains have larger average screen counts at their theaters," he says. "Traditionally, they have a regional film buyer that handles a group of theaters; nowadays they employ a software algorithm that does the work for them." Or as Ben Moss said, "If you have sixteen screens at your theater, you can get *everything* in. The decisions are just margin stuff like whether you get four or five prints of *Avengers*." Bow Tie has to be more careful about its allotment because the circuit averages just over six screens per theater.

A purely algorithmic approach won't work in some cases, however. Asked about the theater mentioned earlier that sold out four screens of *Avengers: Endgame* while two others, showing *Shazam!* and *The Curse of La Llorona*, were half empty, Milgram says the theater managers might have had other reasons than maximizing their take on a weekend to keep the less popular films on display. "*Shazam!* and *The Curse of La Llorona* were likely still performing well enough to justify holding the [virtual film] prints for another week, even though *Avengers* demand was selling out," he says. The logic is that while dedicating all six screens to a single movie might make sense in the very short run, it's unlikely that even a blockbuster can fill an entire multiplex on its second weekend, and so a theater owner who goes all in on the opening is left scrambling to find new content once the initial surge ends.

Moreover, in some cases, even middling films must be kept in theaters for two or more weeks in order to satisfy pre-existing obligations to studios. A failure to live up to those commitments can result in a lack of access to blockbuster fare the next time around. Which is important, because, as Bow Tie's *Endgame* data helped illustrate, it's the "tentpole" movies that truly make or break an exhibitor's balance sheet.

To take another example from the Bow Tie Partners circuit, *Shazam!* led the pack at the Landmark 9 in Stamford during the first weekend in April with a $12,324 gross (out of $26,313 total for the theater as a whole). In that same theater three weeks later, *Avengers* grossed $114,649, with *Curse of La Llorona, Breakthrough,* and *Shazam!* all earning between $1,300 and $1,600. A stunning 96 percent of the theater's $119,192 gross for the period was *Avengers.* For restaurants, bars or stores, a four-fold increase in revenues from one weekend to the next would be extremely unusual. In the movie exhibition business, it's the normal business cycle.

If you go down the list of top twenty-five domestic grossing films for the period from 2010 to 2019, you'll find that every one of them featured established Hollywood stars with their own built-in fan base, and all but five were reboots, remakes, sequels or adaptations of tried and tested franchises. The tentpoles rule.

* * *

The windowless conference room in which Ben Moss and his colleagues met is on the third floor of the Bow Tie Building, located on the same spot that eighty years earlier B.S. Moss had first opened the Criterion Theatre as "The Theatre of Tomorrow." The Moss business occupies the third and fourth floors of the building, sitting atop flagship locations for The Gap, Old Navy, Starbucks, and McDonalds at the intersection of Broadway and Seventh Avenue at West Forty-Fifth Street.

From his office windows, Charley Moss can gaze out south and west onto a Times Square that still lies very much at the center of the North American entertainment universe. Looking past the surviving truss that once held up a block-long Camel cigarettes billboard the size of five tennis courts, he can see the New Amsterdam Theatre, where Disney's *The Lion King* officially capped the Great White Way's transition from porn mall to family fun fair in 1997. Critics decried the new Disneyfied Times Square, but the commercial renaissance in the area has pumped tens of billions of dollars into local properties. On the opposite side of the street sits a Swatch megastore, the New York Marriott Marquis and the TKTS kiosk, where bargain hunters still line up to get discount Broadway tickets.

Out of Charley's north-facing windows, directly across Forty-Fifth Street, the view takes in an especially important landmark, the Lyceum. Built by producer-manager David Frohman in 1903, the Lyceum remains Broadway's oldest continually operational theater. Apart from its every-day role exhibiting plays and musicals, it serves as a Broadway historical brain trust, housing the Shubert Archive's massive trove of documents in Frohman's old offices on the theater's top floor. (Visitors can observe the tiny trap door that Frohman could open to observe plays in progress, and even, as legend has it, wave a handkerchief to a paramour performing on stage.) It was the Lyceum, of course, where Adolph Zukor first exhibited *Les amours de la reine* Élisabeth, and changed the course of motion pictures in America.

It is fitting that the name "Criterion" lives on at many Bow Tie cinemas: even if the original is no longer in operation, its legacy is felt every night in the many east-coast theaters that bear its name, including Criterion Cinemas New Haven, Criterion Cinemas Greenwich Plaza; Criterion Cinemas at Movieland in Richmond, and Criterion Cinemas in Saratoga Springs.

As a mid-tier player with 232 screens and a large cash flow from its Times Square property, Bow Tie is one of the few companies that is both nimble enough to embrace one-off projects, yet sufficiently well-capitalized to negotiate an act of civil reclamation. It has found its own way to continue B.S. Moss's commitment to architecturally interesting movie houses, eschewing the cookie-cutter approach featured by mall-anchored multiplexes in favor of ambitious urban-restoration projects. Its Movieland at Boulevard Square in Richmond is a seventeen-screen facility within the shell of a former locomotive assembly plant. It contains several elements of its pre-movie existence, including tools and locomotive parts found during construction, and a stretch of historic train track unearthed in the parking lot renovation. Two large murals depicting locomotives built at the facility were commissioned to hang in the lobby. A u-shaped bar serves beer and wine. It is very much what B.S. Moss would have considered a beautiful and sumptuous edifice.

The task of carving a movie theater out of an old train factory or elec-trical utility headquarters is of little interest to big chains such as AMC

(8,200 screens), Cinemark (4,600) or Regal (7,300), which tend to take a functional, lowest-possible cost approach to new construction. The same projects lie beyond the capacity of the smallest circuits, which don't have the financial resources, experience, or patience to invest in large, long-term projects built from scratch in up-and-coming markets.

The family tradition inaugurated by B.S. Moss is now in its fourth generation. Just as B.S. inspired Charles, and Charles inspired Charley, Charley has inspired his own son. Ben's older sister, Elizabeth, who remains involved in the family business, but chose to become a schoolteacher and NGO manager instead of working for Bow Tie, says "going to movies was a big part of our life growing up. We would always go out to shows. But even when we were teenagers, it was obvious that Ben and I had different attitudes. I'd be getting into the movie, but Ben would be looking around the theater and he'd be like, 'I gotta tell Dad that Chair 23 in Row D is broken,' or something. He idolized dad, and it surprised no one that he followed him into the business."

Two other Moss family commitments remain alive. First, to the broader community. To this day, Bow Tie Partners raises money and awareness for several charitable enterprises, including: the Michael J. Fox Foundation's campaign to cure Parkinson's Disease, the Variety Children's Charity, the End Allergies Together (EAT) campaign, and the Will Rogers Motion Picture Pioneers Foundation. Second, the Mosses still prefer to keep low media profiles. Despite their extensive entertainment-industry contacts, they both have little interest in celebrity gossip or Hollywood junkets. They tend to keep a safe distance from the self-promoting and often self-destructive egomaniacs who rule Hollywood, choosing instead to live like the corps of anonymous, sober-minded professionals that preceded them at Bow Tie, and that predominate in many other American theater circuits, whether AMC, Regal, or Cinemark. Their leaders are no better known than those at insurance companies. With the single screen, blockbuster promoting theater a thing of the past, such anonymity is easier to manage than ever before.

Being a privately held company also helps reduce the company's profile: the signature projects Charley and Ben have embarked upon would have been difficult to push through the risk-averse committee cultures of typical publicly traded organizations. The idea for Movieland in Richmond originated with a stopover following a father-son motorcycling trip through the Shenandoah Valley. Charley and Ben simply had a hunch about the place. With the big circuits, by contrast, construction and acquisition decisions tend to be based on market data. Mere hunches, no matter how much experience leans behind them, don't get much airtime.

Whether the Bow Tie business continues to expand outside of high-density urban areas, or whether at some point it returns to the great cities, will depend on human migration. In recent years, it had seemed as though the middle-class exiles who fled New York and other centers in the late twentieth-century were beginning to have second thoughts about the suburban lifestyle. They were moving back to the big cities. Covid may now swing the pendulum the other way.

The one sure thing amid all the uncertainty is that people will be going to movies somewhere. For all the change that cinema has undergone, from talkies to blockbusters to television and DVDs and Netflix, the hurry-and-find-your-seat ritual of movie-going remains consistent over the last century of American entertainment. The films themselves have changed enormously, as have aspects of the exhibition technology, but hordes of people still regularly show up at movie theaters, buy their tickets, their popcorn, sit down, and enjoy a film. Film exhibition is holding its own. More than a billion tickets are sold every year.

It will be some time before Ben's own children are old enough to see the adult shows at Moss-owned cinemas. So it's hard to say whether the Moss business will survive into a fifth generation. "Whether I'm around to see a fifth generation eventually take the reins is a question for my doctor," says Charley. "But whatever the fates hold, I hope they have some appreciation of the legacy at stake. Sustaining a family business into the next generation is like planning a film sequel: you should never copy the predecessor outright. But at the very least, examine it closely, so you can understand what made it successful."

Darkness and Light

Abbout halfway through the century-old silent film *Daddy-Long-Legs*, there is a comedic scene that would have been mysterious to most viewers not so long ago, but which now makes perfect sense. An orphan named Judy, played by Mary Pickford, is awarded a scholarship by an enigmatic benefactor. But when the time comes to head off to school, she can't get on the train which is packed with commuters. Suddenly, Pickford sneezes. The whole train car immediately empties, with travelers fleeing in all directions, allowing Pickford to waltz into the car with ease.

The scene is played for laughs, but the background to the joke is anything but funny. This original version of *Daddy-Long-Legs* came out in May 1919, after the Spanish Flu infected a third of the world's population and killed tens of millions, including an estimated 675,000 Americans. Many of the *Daddy-Long-Legs'* actors and production staff would have known victims of the disease. Los Angeles was ravaged in late 1918, with whole studios going dark for months. Among the dead were wunderkind writer and director John Collins, and thirty-one-year-old matinee idol Harold Lockwood, who contracted the disease on set while filming *Shadows of Suspicion*.

Early 2020 has been a strange time to prepare a book on the history of film exhibition because this is the only time in living memory when the simple act of going to a theater and watching a movie has been impossible. Since the industry began, there have been predictions that new technologies would destroy it, whether the emerging threat was radio, television, the VCR, pay-per-view, DVDs, streaming services, smartphones, or flat-screen home theaters. Billions of people have used and enjoyed these technologies, but the prophecies always have been exaggerated. Today's threat comes from COVID-19, not a technology but a virus. Anyone who loves going to the movies hopes this threat, too, is exaggerated.

One might imagine that Charley Moss and his son Ben, now CEO of Bow Tie Cinemas, and their fellow exhibitors would have recognized early the dangers posed to their business by the pandemic, and made plans for closures in the earliest weeks of 2020. But Charley and his colleagues were as surprised as the rest of us when the international lockdown began. "I heard about it as a tragedy that was playing out in China and other foreign countries," he says. "My first definitive sign that this was going to be a serious blow to the industry was when studios started moving their spring and summer films to the fall—especially the new James Bond sequel, which got pushed from April 2020 to the end of the year and beyond."

At first, Charley and his colleagues scrambled to find new content for their theaters. And for a brief time, they discussed curated retrospectives of classic films from the 1940s, 1950s, and 1960s. But by mid-March, these discussions were moot as mayors and governors across the United States ordered theaters shuttered indefinitely. Instead of managing content, Charley and Ben were having difficult conversations with insurers, landlords and employees. The most wrenching aspect was the need to furlough hundreds of front-line theater workers, mostly young people selling popcorn and tickets. Their jobs had ceased to exist, at least for the time being.

The company's exhibition revenue was down to zero, and every means of reducing costs had to be taken. Those costs included monthly rent payments on leased theaters, a subject Charley knew would be a matter of delicate negotiation, and they were–some easier than others.

The earlier pandemic, too, was expected to be fatal to the exhibition industry. "The houses will never recover from the losses they have sustained from the grip epidemic," one prominent film executive told the trade journal *Moving Picture World* in November 1918. Yet just three weeks later, the same publication carried this description of a scene outside a theater that had reopened: "The passing throngs . . . hesitated, still uncertain as to whether or not one huge joke was in the process of being played, walked up to the cashier's cage, and then, satisfied that it was all true, entered joyously . . . By night, moving picture houses downtown and in the residential districts were going full blast . . . Picture exchange managers stood on the sidewalks and rubbed their hands as they watched the files of eager fans pass in. House managers stood just inside the door and registered happiness, their faces wreathed in smiles."

Like the Spanish Flu epidemic, our medical emergency will also pass. Unfortunately for film exhibitors, that's not the whole of the challenge. During the lockdown, and virtually overnight, the exhibitors' traditional suppliers became their competitors. With theaters closed, movie studios doubled down on their investments in their own streaming services. Warner Brothers, for instance, became more reliant on HBO Max, and Disney on Disney+. For the first time in history, home movie viewing gained priority over theater viewing. Disney released its *Mulan* first to streaming audiences, rather than for an exclusive period of time to theaters. Warner released *Wonder Woman 1984* to streaming and in-theater audiences simultaneously. The customary window during which theaters could count on having new Hollywood fare all to themselves appeared to be closing, in no small part because the studios receive all the revenue from streaming services but share the box-office take with cinema owners.

It remains to be seen, post-pandemic, if the exhibition business will regain its central position in the movie industry, or if it will have a reduced presence, or none at all. If the theaters do survive, it will be because there is something about public film viewing that no private form of entertainment can replace. For more than a century now, movies have demonstrated that while people love to be entertained, what they really crave is connection, and not just with friends and family—with society at large.

Think back to 1919, and what it must have been like to be in a crowded theater watching that scene in *Daddy-Long-Legs* with hundreds of strangers, all laughing at once as those on-screen passengers scattered from Pickford.

Everyone in the theater would have known someone who'd been seriously ill with Spanish Flu, maybe even someone who'd died, which is why they all would have instantly recognized the morbid anxiety expressed by the actors. Just six months earlier, they were those people. As with all good observational humor, then and now, the real butt of the joke was the audience itself.

In moments such as this, a movie audience can instantly transform from a group of strangers into a sort of socially bonded collective, with each person's unguarded expression of joy audibly affirming the joy of everyone else (which is why early sitcoms had laugh tracks). Something similar happens during movies that are sad, scary or suspenseful. And a huge part of our common culture is stitched together from thousands of little moments like that, shared with strangers who laugh, cry, scream and gasp with us in the same dark room. You simply can't get that experience in your home.

So there is reason for optimism. Even with the abundance of entertainment available to us, with Netflix, Amazon Prime, Hulu, Disney+ and a dozen other streaming services at our fingertips, there's a good chance that Americans will welcome the first opportunity to return to a comfortable seat in a crowded, darkened theater and the magic that happens when light hits the big screen. For many, it will be that exact moment when this dark and deadly period feels truly behind us.

APPENDIX

T HE HISTORY OF theatrical entertainment can be told in the photos and stories of North America's oldest theater chain, B.S. Moss/ Bow Tie Cinemas. What follows is a basic timeline of the company's holdings, from nickelodeons to vaudeville and movie palaces, and all the way past shopping-center single-screen theaters, multiplexes, and beyond to "the theatre of tomorrow."

Twentieth-century B.S. Moss Theaters

New York

55th Street Playhouse, 154 W. 55th St., New York, NY
The company operated this small, independent film theater in the 1970s. It was built in a former horse stable and had 299 seats.

8th Street Playhouse, 52 W. 8th St., New York, NY
When it first opened in 1929, it was known as the Film Guild Cinema and had 500 seats. Operated by B.S. Moss Enterprises from 1986 to 1988, this famed cinema was home to the New York showing of *The Rocky Horror Picture Show*.

Belair Cinema, 209 W. Merrick Rd., Valley Stream, NY
Built by Charles B. Moss, the Belair opened on June 26, 1963. The 600-seat shopping center theater was later twinned. The theater operated into the 1980s and then was gutted and converted to retail after closing.

Broadway Theatre, 1445 Broadway, New York, NY
This 1,700-seat theater opened in 1888 and was taken over by B.S. Moss in 1908. Moss brought in Keith-Albee Vaudeville and moving pictures, a winning combination that worked until the late 1920s. The Broadway closed on January 2, 1929, and was demolished. Moss took the name "Broadway Theater" and moved it to his Colony Theater, some ten blocks north.

Cameo Theatre, 138 W. 42nd St., New York, NY
B.S. Moss opened his "Salon of the Cinema," a purpose-built movie house, in December 1921. Moss sold the theater to another operator in 1942, who renamed it the Bryant. The 600-seat house lasted until 2006, running adult fare. It was demolished, and the parcel was merged with its neighbors to house the new Bank of America headquarters.

Castle Theatre, Boardwalk and Jackson Boulevard, Long Beach, NY
B.S. Moss opened the Castle on the Boardwalk on June 28, 1923. The 1,400-seat auditorium featured vaudeville and motion pictures. Operated seasonally, the theater was sold five years later, at which point it was operated strictly as a movie theater until it was destroyed by fire in 1936.

Central Theatre, 449 Central Ave., Cedarhurst, NY
The 1,154-seat Central opened in 1923. The company took the theater over in the 1970s, and turned it into a triplex in June 1980, in an attempt to fight new competition. The venerable Central closed in September 1982 and was converted to a shopping mall.

Coliseum Theatre, 4260 Broadway, New York, NY
Located in Manhattan's Washington Heights neighborhood, the B.S. Moss Coliseum was the third largest theater in the United States, with 3,500 seats, when it opened in 1920. Architects Eugene DeRosa and Percival Pereira designed the deluxe house in Adam style. During the golden age of vaudeville, Moss and B.F. Keith brought such famous legends as W. C. Fields, the Marx Brothers, and Eddie Cantor to the huge stage of the Coliseum. RKO acquired the theater from Moss a few years later. Many chains and

independent operators ran the theater, and it closed for the last time in October 2011 as a four-screen theater. All four screens sat approximately 250 each and were all located in the former balcony, as the orchestra level was converted to retail in the 1990s. The prime lot where it stood on the corner of Broadway and 181st St. eventually proved to be too valuable and, as of this writing, demolition of the once beautiful theater has commenced.

Colony Theatre, 1681 Broadway, New York, NY
Famed theater architect Eugene DeRosa designed the roughly 1,800-seat Colony for B.S. Moss, which opened on Christmas Day in 1924. This theater plays an important role in both company history and in the history of cinema. *The Thief of Bagdad*, starring Douglas Fairbanks, was the first movie to play the Colony. In 1928, history was made when B.S. Moss's contemporary and friend, Walt Disney, premiered his first Mickey Mouse cartoon short, *Steamboat Willie*, at the Colony. In 1930 Moss changed the name of the theater to the Broadway and turned it to legitimate bookings. Ten years later, the Broadway was once again a movie house, and Walt Disney premiered his new animated feature, *Fantasia*, at the theater. The very first theatrical stereo system, Fantasound, was installed, and *Fantasia* ran for over a year. Next up was the premiere and long engagement of Disney's *Dumbo*. In 1952, history was made once again when the Broadway became the very first Cinerama theater, with *This Is Cinerama* running for thirty-five weeks. Moss later sold the theater to the Shubert Organization. It is still in operation as a premiere legitimate house and still named the Broadway Theater.

Columbia Theatre, 10-14 Beach 20th St., Far Rockaway, NY
B.S. Moss opened the Colony, just a block south of his Strand Theater, in 1920. The 2,000-seat theater was a prime house on B.F. Keith's vaudeville circuit, and many famous vaudevillians graced the stage of the Columbia. Later sold to RKO, it was demolished in the late 1980s for a parking lot.

Criterion Theatre, 1514 Broadway, New York, NY
Without a doubt the company's flagship and current headquarters, the Criterion opened on September 16, 1936, with Kay Francis in *Give Me Your*

Heart. The house was designed in Art Moderne-style by Eugene DeRosa and Thomas Lamb, and boasted seventeen hundred seats in the first purpose-built movie palace in Times Square. B.S. Moss leased the house to Loews Theatres in the fall of 1938 but took the theater back in 1949 to comply with antitrust legislation, as Loews owned Metro-Goldwyn-Mayer at the time. 1953 marked an important date in history, when the Criterion showed *Fort Ti* from Columbia Pictures and became the first theater ever to project a movie in 3-D (with paper glasses), with stereo sound and color by Technicolor. Many major world premieres happed at the theater, including *The Ten Commandments* on November 8, 1956; *Lawrence of Arabia* projected on 70mm film on December 15, 1962; *South Pacific* on March 19, 1958; *My Fair Lady* on October 21, 1964; *Thoroughly Modern Millie* on March 21, 1967; *Funny Girl* on September 19, 1968; and *Patton* on February 5, 1970. In 1979, the theater was twinned by extending the balcony front to the proscenium, creating a new, 1,041-seat house upstairs. In March of 1980, four screens were created in what was former basement retail space. In 1988, Charley Moss entered into a partnership with United Artists Theaters, who took over operation of all the company's holdings at that time. United Artists twinned the 1,037-seat orchestra level house, creating two 400-seat auditoriums. The theater closed as a seven-plex in the spring of 2000 and was gutted to create prime retail space.

Flatbush Theatre, 2207 Church Ave., Brooklyn, NY
The Flatbush opened in 1914 and featured vaudeville, plays, and motion pictures. Later acquired by RKO, the 1,648-seat Flatbush was an early casualty of television and closed in 1952. It was converted to retail space, and still stands.

Franklin Theatre, 887 Prospect Ave., Bronx, NY
With 2,937 seats, the Franklin was one of the largest theaters built by B.S. Moss. Designed by Eugene DeRosa, it opened on September 5, 1921. Moss sold the theater to RKO a few years later. In 1960 it was converted to a supermarket, which was demolished in 1980.

Hamilton Theatre, 3560 Broadway, New York, NY

The 1,857-seat deluxe Hamilton opened in 1913 and was equipped with a Moeller theater pipe organ. The Hamilton was also acquired by RKO later on and converted to a full-time movie palace. Declining neighborhood conditions contributed to the close of the Hamilton in 1960, and the auditorium was later used as a church, a boxing auditorium and a discotheque. Current Bow Tie Cinemas owners and management toured the Hamilton in 2006, hoping to purchase the building to convert to a modern-day multiplex. A deal could not be made, and the theater still sits in derelict condition awaiting its next performance.

Jefferson Theatre, 214 E. 14th St., New York, NY

The Lower East Side surely celebrated the opening of the deluxe Jefferson, when B.S. Moss opened the 1,916-seat theater in 1913. Designed by George Keister and Thomas Lamb, the Jefferson featured a mix of vaudeville and moving pictures. Later acquired by RKO, the theater operated well into the 1970s. It sat vacant and decaying until 2000, when it was demolished for future development.

Madison Theatre, 54-30 Myrtle Ave., Ridgewood, NY

On November 24, 1927, B.S. Moss opened the 2,760-seat Madison with B.F. Keith vaudeville shows and motion pictures. A major house in the company, the Madison was later acquired by RKO. Lasting until the 1970s, the theater was converted to retail and still serves that purpose today.

Malverne Cinema, 350 Hempstead Ave., Malverne, NY

The Kenney Amusement Company opened their theater in May 1947, boasting 688 seats on a single floor. The theater was acquired by B.S. Moss and featured a twelve-seat "cry room" on the mezzanine level next to the projection booth. Decorations at the theater were carried out by the famous Rambusch Company of New York. After Moss's tenure there, the theater was taken over by an independent operator. It currently serves as a popular five-screen premiere art house serving an upscale clientele.

Movieland, 1567 Broadway, New York, NY
The Schubert Brothers opened Times Square's Central Theater in 1913, with seating for eleven hundred. Designed by architect Herbert Krapp in French Renaissance style, its stage was considerably smaller than most other legitimate Broadway theaters, and the theatre had adopted a movies-only policy by 1928. Over the years the theater had several names: the Columbia, the Gotham, the Holiday, the Odeon and the Forum. In October 1980, the Central's name changed once again, becoming Movieland when B.S. Moss Enterprises took the theater over. The biggest win for the single-screen theater was the exclusive Times Square booking of Steven Spielberg's *E.T. The Extra-Terrestrial*, which played for about a year. The company operated the theater until March 1989. The theater later served as a popular nightclub before it was demolished in 1998 for a hotel.

Movieland 8th St., 36 E. 8th St., New York, NY
Thomas Lamb designed the Art Theatre, which opened on October 7, 1940. The Art was operated by many theater chains and closed in 1985 as an RKO Century Warner Theaters location. Charley Moss then leased the theater and converted it to a triplex. The theater was a success and was taken over by United Artists in partnership with B.S. Moss Theaters in 1988. The neighborhood favorite was sold to New York University and, in 1997, NYU converted the theater into the Iris and B. Gerald Cantor Film Center.

Movieland Yonkers, 2548 Central Park Ave., Yonkers, NY
On December 16, 1977, the Moss family debuted Movieland in Yonkers with four screens: a free- standing building located behind a shopping center. One of the opening features was *Close Encounters of the Third Kind*. The theater was an instant success, and two more screens were added soon after. Management was taken over by United Artists in 1988 in partnership with B.S. Moss Theaters. Regal was the final operator of the theater (after they acquired United Artists), when it closed in July 2012. In 2013 it became the first Westchester County theater for the Texas-based Alamo Drafthouse chain and is still in operation today.

Movieworld, 242-02 61st Ave., Douglaston, NY
Located under the parking deck of a shopping center adjacent to the Long
Island Expressway, B.S. Moss opened the seven-screen Movieworld in 1983,
with capacities ranging from 90 to 450 seats in the auditoriums. United
Artists assumed management in partnership with Moss in 1988, and in the
spring of 2004 the theater closed. An independent operator took it over,
followed by another, and the popular multiplex closed on July 3, 2018. It
is still sitting empty as of this writing, but it has been announced that the
theater would be demolished for future retail development.

Park Theater, 4322 5th Ave., Brooklyn, NY
B.S. Moss opened the Park in Brooklyn's Sunset Park neighborhood in
1915. Thomas Lamb designed the 1,308-seat house, which featured a
Wurlitzer organ. Another operator closed the Park in 1965, and it was
converted to a supermarket that is still in operation.

Raceway Cinema, 1020 Old Country Road, Westbury, NY
Architect Robert Kahn designed the 1,850-seat luxury movie house for
Charles B. Moss. Located next to the now long-gone Roosevelt Raceway,
the theater played roadshow reserved seat engagements from the time it first
opened in June 1967. In 1975, the theater became a tennis club and has
since been demolished.

Regent Theatre, 1912 7th Ave., New York, NY
Thomas Lamb designed what is widely considered New York City's first "all
picture" theater in what was then a German American section of Harlem.
The Regent opened in 1913 with the movie *Pandora's Box*, starring silent
film giant John Bunny. Above the proscenium, the mural depicting the surrender of Granada topped off the auditorium, decorated in hues of blue,
gold, and red. The theater was an immediate disaster, and it was taken over
by B.S. Moss. Famed theater impresario Samuel Rothafel, better known as
"Roxy," was brought in to take over management, and Moss added vaudeville acts to augment the screen presentations. In order to drive patronage,
Roxy and Moss decided to move the projection booth to the orchestra

level and install a glass wall behind it so guests could see the machines in operation. These were considered modern marvels at the time, and the projectionists were dressed in all-white uniforms. The theater's fortunes turned, and Roxy moved on to Broadway's Strand Theater. RKO took over the theater and operated it until 1964. It was then sold to an evangelical church, which still is housed in the building. The church has lovingly cared for the building and, in recent years, has been restoring some of the theater's original architectural features.

Riviera Theater, 1060 St. John's Place, Brooklyn, NY
On December 10, 1921, B.S. Moss opened the Riviera. Designed by Eugene DeRosa, the 2,292-seat house boasted a Kimball pipe organ. It was sold to another operator in 1928 and lasted until 1953. The lovely auditorium, decorated in gold and rose, has since been demolished.

Strand Theatre, 714 Beach 20th St., Far Rockaway, NY
With 1,730 seats, the Strand was the largest theater of the handful that once existed on the peninsula that holds Far Rockaway. Later acquired by RKO, the building finally closed in the mid-1970s. The building sat decaying for many years, but recently was converted to an office and retail building.

Tilyou Theatre, 1607 Surf Ave., Brooklyn, NY
Named after the founder of Coney Island's famed Steeplechase Park, Moss opened the Tilyou on March 18, 1926. It was outfitted with a Wurlitzer theatrical pipe organ. The 2,276-seat Tilyou was sold to RKO, who operated it until 1967. The tattered Tilyou sat empty and decaying until 1975, when it was unceremoniously demolished for a parking lot.

Washington Theatre, 1805 Amsterdam Ave., New York, NY
The Washington is the oldest standing theater designed by famed architect Thomas Lamb. It opened on January 21, 1910, and had 1,432 seats. William Fox assumed operation of the theater a few years later, and in 1950 it became a tabernacle which it remained until 2010. At the time of its closing, the theater was substantially intact. The building is sitting awaiting its next curtain call.

Colorado

Movieland, 218 E. Valley Road, Carbondale, CO

Charley Moss constructed the five-screen Movieland, opening it as the Roaring Fork Valley's only multiplex in 1991. The theater was expanded to seven screens a few years later. For a time, Movieland was the only theater that B.S. Moss operated. The theater was remodeled in 2016 and is still in operation.

New Jersey

Lee Theatre, Lemoine Ave., Fort Lee, NJ

The 1,500-seat deluxe Lee opened on October 24, 1951. The orchestra level held eight hundred seats, with the remainder in the balcony. The first feature was *Showboat*, starring Howard Keel. B.S. Moss Enterprises was the only operator of the theater which was closed and demolished in 1973.

Linwood Theatre, 168 Fletcher Ave., Fort Lee, NJ

The Linwood joined the company's portfolio on July 10, 1963. It was part of a shopping center close to the George Washington Bridge. By 1980 United Artists was operating the theater and twinned it. Later in the decade the Linwood closed and was converted into a CVS Drug Store.

Mall Theatre, Bergen Mall, W. Spring Valley Ave., Paramus, NJ

The Mall Theater opened with Peter Sellers starring in *The Mouse That Roared* on June 13, 1960, and was the first-ever indoor theater in Paramus, NJ. Concessions at the time were dispensed from vending machines, which were located in a row in the lobby. One dispensed soft drinks, another popcorn, and of course a candy machine was very popular. The Mall often played exclusive Bergen County engagements of high-end art films. In March 1978, the theater was twinned. Last operated by Cineplex Odeon, the theater closed and was demolished in the late 1980s.

Galaxy Theatre, 7000 Boulevard East, Guttenberg, NJ

Considered a very modern theater when Charles Moss built it in 1977, the Galaxy failed to attract audiences and was closed after only a year in operation, even though it was located in the shopping arcade of a large apartment complex. A decade later it was reopened and failed again. Another operator triplexed the 530-seat Galaxy and instituted a discount policy in the late 1980s, which proved successful. The theater lasted until 2007 and has been converted to office space.

Florida

State Theatre, 506 W. University Ave., Gainesville, FL
In 1945, the State Theater opened as a modern showplace with seating for 825. B.S. Moss operated the State in the late 1950s into the early 1960s before selling its Florida holdings. Another operator took over and ran the State into 2000. It has since been converted to an office supply store.

Ritz Theatre, 1921 Hollywood Blvd., Hollywood, FL
Not much is known about the Ritz, except that it opened in 1925 in downtown Hollywood. Moss only operated it for a few short years in the 1950s, and the building has since been torn down.

Ritz Theatre, 15 E. Silver Spring Blvd., Ocala, FL
The Elta Theater was constructed in 1928 and featured a Wurlitzer organ. In the 1930s, its name was changed to the Ritz and went through a series of operators. B.S. Moss operated it for a decade or so, beginning in the mid-1950s. Later it was known as the Florida Theater. It has been demolished since.

Astor Theatre, 37 W. Pine St., Orlando, FL
Originally called the Grand Theater, the Astor made its debut in the 1920s. The Astor name came in 1953 when Moss took it over. The 720-seat building was torn down in 1960 for a parking lot. B.S. Moss was the last operator.

Twenty-first-century Bow Tie Cinemas

For the last decade of the twentieth century, and the first four years of the twenty-first, B.S. Moss Theaters operated Movieland in Carbondale, CO, only. When that theater was built, in conjunction with the development of the hugely popular Orchard Plaza Shopping Center, there was not much around the area, which was known as "El Jebel." For years the theater's newspaper directory gave the theater's address as "at the Stoplight in El Jebel." The project spawned major development in the El Jebel area, and the theater continues to serve its patrons well.

In the early 2000s, the Moss family decided to jump "head-over-heels" back into the movie theater business, and purchased a beautiful but derelict building in downtown New Haven, CT. The building was developed into forty-four luxury apartments (known as Temple Square) and a five-screen movie theater, which was expanded twice quickly after it opened.

This part of the history of the theater circuit is written from first-hand knowledge, and is formatted differently from the theatres of the previous century.

Criterion Cinemas, 80 Temple St., New Haven, CT (2004)
Downtown New Haven celebrated its first new theater in over thirty years when the company, now called Bow Tie Cinemas, ceremoniously opened its luxurious new Criterion Cinemas at the corner of Temple and George streets. The theater's grand opening was held on November 5th, with the Fox Searchlight picture *Sideways* on two of its five screens. Seating for the five screens was as follows, in order of cinema number: 215, 164, 164, 141, and 185.

The décor, designed by New York City architect Rich Furman, is first class. Gold metal ceilings, gilded columns, and custom Bow Tie carpeting gives patrons the feel of premium movie going, augmented by a large screen-printed mural of historic photos from the family's rich theatrical history. Stars from the many premieres held at the Criterion in New York City are featured, along with a photo of the "glass projection booth" described in the 20th Century section that B.S. Moss installed in its Regent Theater in

Manhattan as a gimmick. To honor his grandfather, Charley Moss decided to put a glass wall in the projection booth of Theaters 2 and 3 at the new theater, showing patrons a modern-day film projection system.

The company trademarked its motto, "Returning Style and Elegance to the Movie Going Experience®." It was also the first theater in Connecticut to have a liquor license, and the first to serve real butter on its signature popcorn.

The theater struggled at first, due to a firm clamp on first-run bookings in that zone held by Moss competitor National Amusements, which had theaters surrounding downtown New Haven. That clearance had been the subject of unsuccessful legal action by another downtown operator of an ailing three-screen art house known as the York Square Cinemas.

Great, long-standing relationships between the Moss family and the studios led to an eventual wearing down of that clearance. The Criterion celebrated with its first "day-and-date" booking with the National Amusements location in Orange, CT, by playing *Cinderella Man* (2005) from Universal Pictures, and marking the first time a first-run commercial motion picture played in downtown New Haven in many years. The success of that booking led another studio, Walt Disney, to book *Pirates of the Caribbean: Dead Man's Chest* (2006) into the Criterion. National Amusements balked and pulled the booking from its theaters, and the Criterion enjoyed huge success by playing it on three screens. In 2006, the company decided to take some space in the building originally reserved for a restaurant and create Theaters 6 (164 seats) and 7 (141 seats).

In the fall of 2006, 20th Century Fox booked the film *Borat* into the Criterion. National Amusements once again pulled their runs of the film. The Criterion grosses, thanks to sellouts from Yale University, were huge. National Amusements started the film on its second week of release in their area theaters, and the booking clearance was forever broken.

In 2009, another smaller space, which had originally been thought perfect for a pub-style operation, was earmarked for two private screening rooms. These spaces weren't large enough for a traditional movie projection system, so they were outfitted with small digital projectors and opened showing off-beat independent and foreign product that was available on blu-ray or DVD. Those two screening rooms, Theaters 8 (originally 28 seats, now 42) and 9 (35 seats) have been successful. Theater 8 was expanded by eliminating a party/function room that was constructed adjacent to it but saw little action.

The Criterion has continued to run top-quality first-run commercial and independent films on its nine screens to this day. Its bar offerings were expanded in 2019 from beer and wine to the full bar experience, and some kitchen equipment was added.

Crown Theatres, acquisition (2006)

On November 12, 2006, the company expanded rapidly with the acquisition of twelve theater locations from Crown Theaters, based in South Norwalk, CT. This acquisition catapulted Bow Tie Cinemas into a role as a major regional player, and the company established a home office in South Norwalk, CT, above the Regent Theater. In March 2007, the office moved to the company's Ridgefield 7 Office Building located in Ridgefield, CT, where it remains as of 2019.

The locations acquired from Crown:

Criterion Cinemas at Greenwich Plaza, 2 Railroad Ave., Greenwich, CT
The 690-seat Plaza was opened by the Brandt family's Trans-Lux Theaters in 1970 as the single-screen Plaza Theater. By 1983 it was operating as a triplex. Bow Tie took over the theater and changed its bookings from strictly commercial product to a mix of upscale commercial and art film titles to better compete with the newer theater in neighboring Port Chester, NY. It was a successful move by the company, and the theater's name was officially changed to Criterion Cinemas at Greenwich Plaza. The large Theater 1 features a huge screen, 434 seats, and an Australian-style waterfall grand drape. As of 2019, the strip center's landlord is looking to redevelop the entire block which would create a new, modern theater at the opposite end of where the triplex is now. The proposed new cinema would have six or seven screens and would operate as a "Bow Tie Ultimate" location, featuring plush reclining seats, a full bar, and expanded dining options.

Ultimate Majestic 6 & BTX Theater, 118 Summer St., Stamford, CT
This popular theater opened in 1996 to complement Crown's nearby Landmark 9. Its largest auditorium featured 460 seats and was equipped with George Lucas' THX sound system. On November 15, 2019, Bow Tie will celebrate the complete remodeling of the Majestic into the "Ultimate Majestic 6," with the opening of the company's first large sit-down bar, remodeled auditoriums with luxury reclining seats, and full dining options. The largest auditorium described above has been reimagined into one of the company's premium large format houses, known as BTX—Bow Tie X-Treme®. The BTX house features 183 luxury recliners, a significantly larger screen than the previous theatre, and Dolby Atmos® 13.1 surround sound.

Landmark 9, 5 Landmark Square, Stamford, CT
The Trans-Lux Twin first opened in 1970, with two houses seating four hundred and twelve hundred people, respectively, on the second floor of an office complex attached to the Stamford Town Center mall. A third screen was added in a former restaurant space adjacent to the theater, creating a 100-seat house. A few years later, the 1200-seat house was divided into four smaller screening spaces, seating between 150 and three hundred people. In 1996, Crown Theaters created three cinema spaces on the ground floor, along with a new box office and manager's office, and a complete remodel of the six screens on the second floor. Bow Tie Cinemas plans to renovate the Landmark 9 in 2020.

New Canaan Playhouse, 89 Elm St., New Canaan, CT
The Playhouse Operating Company premiered their deluxe new theater on September 19, 1923, serving posh New Canaan. At some point, then-operator United Artists "twinned" the theater and gave up most of the stadium space and original projection booth in the back of the auditorium to create rental space. New rest rooms were created on the ground floor in a former retail store that was annexed onto the small lobby, and the projection booth was moved forward. Bow Tie reseated the theater and replaced the concession stand in the fall of 2010, and again activated what was accessible of the former stadium area at the back of Theater 2, adding sixteen

more seats to the house. This charming little theater continues to please the town's inhabitants.

Wilton Cinema 4, 27 River Road, Wilton, CT
Hoyts Theaters of Australia, a major cinema operator in the Northeast from the late 1980s to mid-2000s, constructed the four-screen theater attached to a new shopping center in 2000. Two houses seat 186; the other two each seat 147. The theater boasts large screens and is still operated by Bow Tie as of 2019.

Ultimate Regent 8, 64 North Main St., Norwalk, CT
The Regent was an exciting new development in 1995, creating an eight-screen theater, retail and office space out of combined former supermarket space and new construction. The theater sparked major redevelopment in the previously derelict South Norwalk area, with the blossoming of many new restaurants and retail spaces. The area continues to deliver, and in August 2017 the Regent became Bow Tie's first "Ultimate" theater, offering reserved recliner seating, food and full bar.

Ultimate Royale 6, 542 Westport Ave., Norwalk, CT
Located a few miles away from the Regent on the Norwalk/Westport border, the Royale first opened in 1996 with similar décor as the Majestic in Stamford. In October 2017, the Royale was christened as the second "Ultimate" location following a major renovation. It is also the home of the company's first Jack and Harry's Popcorn location. The staff creates several different sweet and savory flavors of popcorn, with caramel and cheddar being the most popular. Jack and Harry's Popcorn made at the Royale serves the company's Ultimate Regent, and both Stamford and Criterion Greenwich locations as well.

Ultimate Marquis 16 & BTX Theater, 100 Quarry Rd., Trumbull, CT
Crown first opened this successful multiplex in 1990 as a ten-screen theater. In 1994, six more screens were added, which were different from the first ten. The original house featured sloped floor seating, while the new six

screens featured stadium-style seating. Bow Tie has remodeled this theater twice: the first time was in 2013, when they added a new concession stand, hot food menu and a remodeled lobby. In 2018 the theater was converted to "Ultimate," with reserved leather recliners, expanded food and a full bar. The original houses were all converted to stadium seating in this remodel, and the largest house was converted into a large-format house with Dolby Atmos® 13.1 surround sound.

Palace 17, 330 New Park Ave, Hartford, CT

Crown opened this giant building in 2000, featuring an early competitor to IMAX® known as Odyssey, which projected 70mm film on a 60-by-80 foot screen. The all stadium-seated theater had three concession stands and three sets of restrooms. Bow Tie added a hot food menu to the theater and in 2010, with the loss of its successful Cinema City art theater nearby, converted one wing to become "Cinema City at the Palace." That wing was decorated with photographs of the original theater and offered an array of coffee drinks at the small concession stand in that area.

Cinema City—235 Brainard Rd., Hartford, CT

Hartford's premiere art house was the highest grossing venue of its type between New York and Boston. Appreciated by audiences from a large area because of excusive access to this type of product, the houses were heavily occupied. Theaters 1 and 4 seated 450 each, and the other two seated 250 apiece. The theater first opened in 1972 and was Hartford's first multiplex. Later in its life, as more competition developed around it, the product was changed a strict art film policy. The Metropolitan Water District made an offer to the landlord to take the property in 2010, and Bow Tie was bought out of its lease there. The venerable Cinema City was demolished for an office building for the utility.

Ultimate Annapolis Mall 11 and BTX Theater, 1020 Westfield Annapolis Mall Rd., Annapolis, MD

Located on the second floor above the food court of a hugely successful regional shopping mall, this theater made its debut in 2000 with houses seating from 460 to 110. It replaced an older quadplex on the first level of the mall, and was a huge success out of the gate. Over the years, Bow Tie replaced the carpeting and auditorium drapes. In 2018 the theater was as a "Bow Tie Ultimate" location, with reserved recliners, food and bar, and new décor.

Harbour 9, 2474 Solomons Island Rd., Annapolis, MD
Located on the second floor of a successful shopping plaza, about one and a half miles from the Westfield Mall, the Harbour made its debut around 1990. For a decade it was the largest theater in the Annapolis market until the opening of the Mall 11. Once that theater made its premiere, the Harbour was relegated to "move over" bookings, second-rate product, and art fare. Soon after Bow Tie took over, the theater was treated more fairly in the zone and was booked with better product. In 2018, electric leather recliners were put in and reserved seating was instituted. A complete remodel was accomplished but no additional food or bar were added, primarily due to space limitations.

Movieland, 400 State St., Schenectady, NY (2007)
Carrying on the tradition of honoring the company's past theaters by using their names, Movieland in downtown Schenectady had its gala opening on May 18th of that year. Designed by architect Kevin Cowan of Kansas City, the theater boasts 1435 seats in stadium-seated auditoriums, a lobby café where guests consume beer, wine and cider, elevated food offerings, and real butter served over signature popcorn. The theater was the first movie theater to operate in downtown Schenectady proper since the 1970s.

Criterion Cinemas at Blue Back Square, 42 S. Main St., West Hartford, NY (2007)
The first new theater in West Hartford to operate since the 1970s, the six-screen cinema is part of the Blue Back Square project that transformed West Hartford from a boutique shop area to a major shopping destination. The theater opened on November 2, 2007, and featured 1,137 seats. Architect Michael Mahaffey of Oklahoma City designed the project. In 2016, the

theater was sold as a package of five locations to Mexican theater operator Cinepolis. It was operating as Cinepolis West Hartford as of 2019.

American Theater, 1450 East Ave., Bronx, NY (2008)
Designed using an art nouveau style by famed theater architect John Eberson, the American premiered as part of the Parkchester development on December 26, 1940. Loews Theatres operated the theater from the time it opened until the time it closed it as a twin-screen operation in the early 1980s. After their tenancy, a series of independent operators ran the American, until it finally closed with the once grand auditorium divided into seven screens in April 2008. Bow Tie reopened the theater and added a new concession stand, new seating and expanded food offerings. The theater limped along until the nearby fourteen-screen Whitestone Multiplex cinemas closed. The American enjoyed a spike in business, but a clause in Bow Tie's lease with the landlord had a provision for retail tenancy. The landlord exercised that option and Bow Tie's last day at the venerable American was in September 2013. The specular lobby and all theater fixtures were gutted and the building reopened as a Marshall's clothing store.

Movieland at Boulevard Square, 1301 N. Boulevard, Richmond, VA (2009)
The company's most ambitious project to date debuted on February 27, 2009. The seventeen-screen Movieland was constructed within the shell of a former locomotive assembly plant that last operated as a steel facility. Auditorium sizes range from 290 to 112. The base building was designed by Commonwealth Architects of Richmond, with design and décor by Michael Mahaffey. Mahaffey created several historical elements, including an exterior sculpture garden of steel rescued from the conversion of the building, a mural of historic tools and various locomotive parts found during the construction, and a stretch of historic train track unearthed in the parking lot renovation. Other buildings on the property include a former brass foundry used for storage at the time of purchase (see Criterion Cinemas at Movieland), and a recycling sorting facility that was demolished for expanded parking. The projection booth was left open in the vast lobby so guests could see the film platter systems in operation. When these were

replaced just a few years later by digital projection systems, the feature lost most of its effect. Two large murals depicting locomotives that were built at the facility were commissioned and hang in the lobby. A u-shaped bar was added, originally serving beer and wine. A tenth anniversary celebration was held on February 27, 2019, and the company celebrated by launching an expanded full bar. From its time of opening, the theater was an instant success and quickly became the top grossing theater in the Richmond market—a position that it still holds in late 2019.

Reston Town Center 11 & BTX, 11940 Market St., Reston, VA (2011)
In 1990, the large development of residential, office, retail and restaurant space opened featuring an eleven-screen theater first operated by National Amusements. They split the original Theaters 1 and 2 into four smaller screening spaces, bringing the total screen count to thirteen. The theater chugged along for years and was taken over by Rave Cinemas in 2011. Two years later, on April 1, 2013, Bow Tie Cinemas took over the operation of the run-down multiplex. The company quickly commenced a large-scale remodel of the theater, restoring the original eleven-screen configuration with stadium seating and leather rockers, adding new concession stands, a beer and wine café, new restrooms, and all new décor on the two-floor operation. The largest house was converted to a large-format BTX cinema. In February 2019, the bar was converted to full bar once Virginia's liquor laws were relaxed, which then allowed guests to take their beverages into their auditorium to enjoy while watching their movie. Bow Tie plans a conversion to "Ultimate" in 2020.

Criterion Cinemas at Movieland, 1330 North Boulevard, Richmond, VA (2012)
In 2012, the former brass foundry space (see Movieland at Boulevard Square, referenced above) was converted into a charming four-screen art house with seating for 97, 44, 44, and 77 in its deluxe houses. The conversion was designed by Christiano Pereira of CPA Architecture in West New York, NJ. Theaters 1 and 4 feature exterior historic windows, so a room-darkening automated drapery system was installed that blocks exterior

lighting in those theaters prior to each show, and opens again at the conclusion. An instant hit, the theater became even more popular when Regal
Cinemas closed their historic Westhampton 1 & 2, the area's long-standing
premiere art house. That title now belongs to the innovative Criterion
Cinemas®.

Clearview Cinemas, acquisition (2013)

On June 13, 2013, Bow Tie Cinemas completed its most ambitious acquisition to date, with the closing of the asset purchase of Clearview Cinemas.
Clearview was originally formed in the 1990s by the owner of the Clearview
Baking Company, A. Dale "Bud" Mayo, and was based in Madison (later
Chatham), NJ. The circuit was cobbled together by combining theaters
that chains were giving up, and smaller in-town theaters that independent
operators sold to them. Most locations were poorly multiplexed. Mayo
sold the chain to Long Island–based cable tv operator Cablevision. During
their ownership, Clearview's locations were offered for years as a benefit
for their subscriber's rewards program. If a customer subscribed to cable,
phone, and internet service, Cablevision rewarded them with two free tickets every Tuesday to the Clearview Cinema of their choice, and discounted
ticket incentives for other days of the week. This led to a great downfall for
Clearview's locations, which were not well maintained. Bow Tie endeav-
ored to overcome this huge obstacle to success by quickly embarking on an
upgraded maintenance program and general deep cleaning. Digital projection and sound upgrades were added to compensate for poor presentation
that plagued many of the locations. Many of the theaters were spun off by
Bow Tie over the years and, to save space, only significant details for certain
theaters are added in the list that follows.

The acquired theaters, which Bow Tie began operating in June 2013,
include the following:

Babylon Cinemas, 34 W. Main St., Babylon, NY
A triplex theater, closed September 7, 2014, by Bow Tie, property sold: now
a legitimate theater known as the Argyle Theater.

Bedford Playhouse, 643 Old Post Rd., Bedford, NY
A twin historic house from 1947 that Bow Tie closed at the end of its lease on January 4, 2015; now reopened as a non-profit triplex.

Bronxville Cinemas, 84 Kraft Ave., Bronxville, NY
One of the jewels of the acquisition, the charming three-screen theater is an owned property and features several small retail spaces and a large recording studio that the company leases out. Located across from the Metro-North train station, the theater first opened in 1926 with 1,116 seats. A fire in 1960 destroyed the interior, and it was rebuilt and reopened. In the 1980s, then-operator United Artists triplexed the theater.

Central Plaza Cinemas, 2630 Central Park Ave., Yonkers, NY
It is ironic that Bow Tie took over what was once B.S. Moss' largest rival in Yonkers, as it is right next door to the company's former Movieland the-atre in that area. The huge, 2500-seat Central Plaza Cinema was opened by General Cinema on December 28, 1966. The theater was twinned, triplexed, and finally turned into a four-screen operation: two large, 600-seat houses were downstairs; the two created out of the former balcony housed 250 each; and the lobby fountain was covered over with hollow flooring. Bow Tie only operated it for a few months, closing it at lease-end on September 19, 2013. The theater has since been converted to retail.

Chelsea Cinemas, 260 W. 23rd St., New York, NY
What was then Manhattan's largest multiplex opened on July 14, 1989. Canada's Cineplex Odeon was the first operator, and Clearview later took over. Bow Tie embarked on an ambitious renovation in 2014, adding luxury leather rockers, new décor, and new concessions. Bow Tie continued the successful run of *The Rocky Horror Picture Show* there, and classic weekly screenings hosted by a female impersonator known as "Hedda Lettuce." In July 2016, the Chelsea Cinemas was part of a five-location package that was sold to Mexico's Cinepolis.

Fine Arts Cinemas, 34 Main St., New City, NY
Bow Tie immediately changed the name from New City Cinema 6, and changed the booking policy to an art-house format upon acquisition, to try to revive this theater. Regal recently had constructed a new multiplex close by. This initiative did not meet with much success and Bow Tie gave up the lease in 2017. An independent operates now this facility, which goes by the name of New City Cinemas.

Franklin Square Cinemas, 989 Hempstead Turnpike, Franklin Square, NY
This 795-seat, six-screen location first opened in 1941 as a single theater. Its screen count varied over the years. One auditorium was created on the former stagehouse of the theater, and another in former retail space. The original house hosts four screens. Bow Tie divested itself of this location in late 2019.

Grand Avenue Cinemas, 1841 Grand Ave., Baldwin, NY
This five-screen theater was built as a single theater, and poorly divided some years later. In November 2014, Bow Tie was able to terminate its lease early, and another operator took the theater over. Bow Tie did not add digital projection to this low-grossing location.

Herricks Cinemas, 3324 Hempstead Turnpike, New Hyde Park, NY
The Herricks opened in the 1960s behind a strip mall. It has been converted to four screens.

Mount Kisco Cinemas, 144 Main St., Mount Kisco, NY
This theater replaced another theater nearby that burned down. The auditorium configuration was changed, and the theater now houses five small screens with 466 seats between them.

Larchmont Playhouse, 1975 Palmer Ave., Larchmont, NY
In 1935, the charming Larchmont Playhouse debuted as the hub of entertainment in this upscale village. It enjoyed most of its life as a 600-seat single screen operation, until Clearview converted it to a triplex. During

that conversion, the original proscenium that was for years draped over was uncovered and restored. Located only one and a half miles away from a thriving eighteen-screen Regal operation, the Larchmont could no longer compete, and Bow Tie quietly exited upon expiration of the lease on September 25, 2016. The theater is still vacant but is owned by Charles Cohen, who purchased the Landmark Theatres chain. The playhouse is awaiting its next incarnation.

Mamaroneck Playhouse, 243 Mamaroneck Ave., Mamaroneck, NY
Located on a thriving street filled with restaurants and shops, the once stately Mamaroneck Playhouse could no longer compete as it was book-ended by competition. The Playhouse Operating Company first opened the Tudor-style Mamaroneck in 1927 and was acquired by United Artists some years later with many original features still intact. Walled off but accessible through one door is the large vaudeville stage, which still had its asbestos fire curtain hanging when Bow Tie took over. There are also twelve abandoned dressing rooms and a fully trapped and rigged stage remaining. On April 27, 2014, Bow Tie closed and mothballed the theater, which for years had not been competitive. It was not converted to digital projection prior to closing. Bow Tie sold the building to another operator, who as of 2019 is in the process of gutting the entire facility to turn it into a dine-in, eight-screen theatrical enterprise.

Manhasset Cinemas, 430 Plandome Rd., Manhasset, NY
This lovely playhouse first opened 1927. The auditorium was later carved up into three screens by United Artists Theaters. Competition developed over the years, and Clearview met with some success by switching to an art film policy. As this was an owned property, Bow Tie sold it and leased it back for a short time. The new owner found a long-term operator, and Bow Tie vacated on April 11, 2019.

Port Washington Cinemas, 116 Main St., Port Washington, NY
The Beacon Theater first opened on October 15, 1927, and boasted a Wurlitzer pipe organ. In the early 1970s it underwent a triplexing; later the balcony was split into two creating a quadplex. An independent operator

took over from United Artists, added a screen on the old vaudeville stage, and two very poor tiny screening rooms carved out of a small retail store. Clearview took over in 1995. This theater suffered a great deal from a lack of convenient parking, and its losses could no longer be tolerated. Bow Tie negotiated out of a long-term lease and closed the theater on January 28, 2018. Its next life awaits.

Roslyn Cinemas, 20 Tower Place, Roslyn, NY
Across from the town's landmark clock tower sits the Roslyn Cinemas, built in 1941. The theater was twinned and triplexed over the years, and finally converted to a four-screen operation. Bow Tie continued the art policy inherited from Clearview. It was sold to the same developer that purchased the Manhasset location, and Bow Tie exited on April 11, 2019. An independent now operates the Roslyn.

Squire Theater, 115 Middle Neck Rd., Great Neck, NY
Opening around 1935, the Squire was designed in Tudor-style and was built directly across from the town's Playhouse Theater. United Artists was a long-term tenant in this building, and their East Coast headquarters was located on the second floor for a period. An independent took over in the 1980s and then Clearview, who divided it into seven screens, including one in a former storefront off the lobby. Bow Tie operated this location until March 31, 2019, when it was passed to an independent.

Ziegfeld Theatre, 141 W. 54th St., New York, NY
The Walter Reade Organization opened Manhattan's last deluxe large movie theater on December 17, 1969, with 1,131 seats. As part of the asset purchase agreement, Bow Tie only managed this theater on behalf of Cablevision as it could not tolerate the theater's immense losses. Through the 1980s, the Ziegfeld enjoyed exclusive motion picture engagements and was very successful. In the 1990s, when larger multiplexes opened in Times Square, it no longer enjoyed that exclusivity and was no longer a viable operation. Premieres and events continued to help the Ziegfeld limp along until Cablevision negotiated out of the lease and on January 28, 2016 the

Ziegfeld closed after the last showing of *Star Wars: The Force Awakens*. The theater has been converted into a two-level ballroom and event space, and retains the Ziegfeld name and marquee.

Beacon Hill 5, 343 Springfield Ave., Summit, NJ
This was Clearview's first new build when it opened on the basement level of a former department store on July 7, 1997. The auditoriums were very small, and the presentation was not top-notch; still, the Beacon Hill served its purpose. As retail operations command higher rents than theaters, the landlord proposed a buyout that Bow Tie accepted, and the theater showed its last movie on February 21, 2016.

Bellevue Cinema 4, 260 Bellevue Ave., Upper Montclair, NJ
The Bellevue premiered on May 13, 1922, in a converted horse stable. The Tudor-style building fits in with most of the buildings in tony Upper Montclair. United Artists split this once-charming house into four screens, stripping it of all of architect John Phillips's décor. On November 12, 2017, at the conclusion of its lease, Bow Tie closed the Bellevue. It is in the process of being converted to a not-for-profit movie theater operation backed by several celebrities who live in the area. Reopening is expected in 2020.

Bergenfield Cinema 5, 58 S. Washington Ave., Bergenfield, NJ
The 1,200-seat Palace opened in the early 1920s with vaudeville and movies. It eventually switched to an all-film policy and was run by United Artists for a time. It was Clearview's second theater operation and was divided by them into five screens, with two under the balcony and two in the former balcony. The fifth was created by constructing a projection room on the stage, throwing an image into a new screen constructed in the auditorium. Seats were added on the stage and into the very front of the house, looking out onto the new screen. A lot of original décor survives, including the ceiling dome, proscenium, and wall detail. The theater's original ball room is still completely intact on the second floor and functions as a dance studio. Bow Tie sold the property to a new owner and ceased theater operations on April 2, 2018. The theater is now operated by an independent.

Bernardsville Cinema 3, 5 Mine Brook Rd., Bernardsville, NJ
The Liberty Theater opened in 1921, with seating for four hundred in this upscale town. In 1970, it was renamed the Bernardsville Cinema. Clearview took over in the 1990s and divided the small theater into three screens, creating a new projection booth on the front of the now-abandoned balcony. Bow Tie's lease expired on November 15, 2019, and the theater operation was assumed by another venture.

Caldwell Cinema 4, 317 Bloomfield Ave., Caldwell, NJ
The Caldwell opened in 1913 as the town's first theater. It survived into the 1950s, but competition from the neighboring Park Theater and television proved too much, and the theater shuttered. It served as a clothing factory for many years. The Park burned down in the 1980s, leaving the town with a single screen operation in a nearby shopping center that had opened in the 1960s. That theater closed eventually, and the Caldwell was revived and reconstructed as a new four-screen multiplex. A radius restriction prohibited the original developer from operating the theater, as he sold some nearby locations to Clearview. In turn, Clearview sued and leased the Caldwell from that developer. In 2018, a devastating flood destroyed the interior of the theater and many other businesses in town. Bow Tie revamped the theater with an all-new concession stand, lobby, and redesigned auditoriums with reclining seating. The capacities are very small, as recliners each take up the space of approximately four traditional theater seats. The luxurious theater made its debut on December 21, 2018, and Bow Tie still operates the Caldwell as of 2019.

Clairidge Cinemas, 486 Bloomfield Ave., Montclair, NJ
The Clairidge first opened in 1922 as a deluxe movie palace designed by architect Nathan Harris. Its mighty Wurlitzer organ plays to this day at the Paramount Theater in Middletown, NY, and was moved there after the Clairidge was multiplexed. In the 1960s, the single-screen Clairidge became New Jersey's first Cinerama theater. On May 13, 1983, a metal box was built into the sumptuous auditorium and three screens were constructed within it. The metal box concealed all the splendor of the Clairidge, but a

small hatch in the projection booth leads you to the roof of the metal box where the original theater sits, largely intact and mostly hidden. The triplex itself was then triplexed, creating six auditoriums in a very unusual layout. Policy was changed to art-film bookings, and the theater business spiked. Bow Tie installed digital projection, which solved the terrible projection issues resulting from the bad chop-job. The highly successful premiere art house is still operated by Bow Tie in 2019.

Closter Cinemas, 19 Vervalen St., Closter, NJ
Another 1960s shopping-center theater, the single-screen Closter opened on July 31, 1963, with Charlton Heston in *55 Days at Peking.* It was one of the first Clearview locations in the 1980s and was then divided into four screens. In January 2016, Bow Tie exited when its lease ran out. CMX Cinemas gutted, rebuilt and reopened the theater in January 2018.

Hoboken Cinemas, 405-415 14th St., Hoboken, NJ
On October 23, 2009, Clearview opened the last new build that it created. Situated on two levels, the five screen theater features three stadium and two sloped floor auditoriums. A second level concession stand was abandoned by Clearview and walled off by Bow Tie once it took over. The theater is not located in the heart of Hoboken's thriving dining and shopping district and suffers from difficult parking. In 2019 business picked up nicely when the nearby sixteen-screen National Amusements Edgewater Multiplex closed its doors. In 2020, the Hoboken will be the first New Jersey home for the prestigious TriBeCa Film Festival.

Kinnelon Cinemas, 25 Kinnelon Rd., Kinnelon, NJ
This eight-plex was shoehorned into a former department store and opened on April 24, 1992. On November 11, 2016, Bow Tie transitioned this theater to a new operator.

Madison Cinema 4, 14 Lincoln Place, Madison, NJ
In 1925, the Madison Theater debuted with 946 seats. The lobby had some marble features, and each restroom had a smoking lounge. Seating was

provided in a traditional style auditorium with a raised stadium area in the rear. Clearview took over in December 1981, and divided the charming Madison into a four-screen operation. Bow Tie exited after a period of month-to-month operation in 2017. Two years later, the theater is still there, with a proposal to demolish and replace it with apartment and retail development. To appease the petitioners that are lobbying to save it, the developer is proposing to add two screens in the new project.

Mansfield Cinema 14, 1965 Route 57, Hackettstown, NJ
In the spring of 1999, Clearview opened this new theater, with fifteen small auditoriums, in a former Jamesway department store. A few years later, two tiny houses were combined to make one medium auditorium. At that time, the theatre was renovated to install stadium seating in thirteen of the fourteen auditoriums. Bow Tie sold this theater in June 2013 to Cinepolis, as part of a five-theater package.

Middlebrook Galleria Cinemas, 1502 Route 35, Ocean Township, NJ
Located behind a shopping center, the theater originally opened in October 1994 with ten screens. It suffered from competition from a fifteen-screen competitive location located a short distance away in a regional shopping mall. Bow Tie successfully exited the theater on October 24, 2014. An independent took over, and the theater closed again. It remains closed at the end of 2019.

Red Bank Twin, 36 White St., Red Bank, NJ
Music Makers Theaters converted a hardware store into a two-screen operation, which opened to the public on March 31, 1971. Clearview took over the operation from Loews Theaters in the 1990s and changed the policy to strictly art-house bookings. Meeting with success, the policy continues to this day under Bow Tie's management. The theater is home to several film festivals and serves the town of Red Bank well.

South Orange Cinemas, 1 SOPAC Way, South Orange, NJ
In 2006 the town of South Orange constructed this project, featuring a 450-seat performing arts center and a five-screen movie theater. Both

operations share a common lobby. The two larger auditoriums are situated on the ground level, and three more sit on the third floor. Rich Furman, who designed Bow Tie's Criterion New Haven was the architect, and the theater opened on November 3, 2006. Bow Tie reseated the auditoriums in 2017.

Strathmore Cinemas, 1055 State Route 34, Aberdeen, NJ
Opened as the Matawan Twin Cinema by an independent operator on December 22, 1971, the Strathmore had seating for 550. Clearview took over in the 1990s, divided each house, and christened their remodeled operation the Strathmore Cinema 4. Seating was reduced to 480 in the four houses. At the end of August 2019, Bow Tie's lease was up. It has been announced that the theater will be reborn as a brew pub.

Parsippany Cinema 12, 3065 Route 46, Parsippany, NJ
On December 22, 1994, Nelson-Ferman Theaters opened their crudely built twelve-plex behind the Morris County Shopping Center. An instant hit, the theater continued until new competition in the Rockaway Mall tore into its business. Bow Tie sold this theater as part of a five-theater package to Cinepolis, a Mexican theater operator.

Succasunna Cinema 10, 21 Sunset Strip, Succasunna, NJ
A single screen operation first known as Cinema 10 (on Route 10) opened in the 1960s. By the end of the 1970s, it had been twinned. Later, the twin was split into four screens. A separate entrance with two flat-floor, upper-level theaters were added then as well. The owner was playing adult films in those two theaters, and had some blowback from the studios about their films playing in the original four houses. The owner then cut a doorway to the upstairs houses. Later, they added four more screens and a new entrance, lobby, and concession stand. Cinema 10 was now truly ten screens. Clearview added a new structure to the building and closed the upstairs houses. Bow Tie sold this theater to Cinepolis as part of a five-theater package.

Tenafly Cinema 4, 4 ½ W. Railroad Ave., Tenafly, NJ
Located across from Tenafly's historic train station (which now functions as retail space, given trains no longer service the borough), the Tenafly Theater opened as a playhouse in 1915. In 1926 it was rebuilt as a film-only theater and was renamed the Bergen. In the 1980s the Bergen became the very first Clearview Cinema. It was divided into four screens and renamed the Tenafly Cinema 4. Screen one still looks very original and features original chandelier lighting and proscenium. An owned property, the Tenafly still serves its patrons with upscale commercial, family, and art product.

Warner Theater, 190 E. Ridgewood Ave., Ridgewood, NJ
In 1932, Warner Brothers Theater Management opened the Warner. The art deco theater was designed by Thomas Lamb and featured an array of dazzling designs. It is very similar to the Warner in Torrington, CT. The large asymmetrical tower on the façade still stands, sans a large, vertical "WARNER" blade sign, which was removed in the 1980s in a decayed state. The marquee currently on the building dates from the early 1960s, although the neon has been removed since it is no longer permitted by the town. In 1978 the theater was twinned by RKO Century Warner Theaters, which was operating it at the time. Cineplex Odeon bought that chain and, on May 23, 1984, the Warner premiered as a four-screen operation. At that time, the whole stunning ceiling was concealed; however, the deco walls in the auditoriums remain. Behind the screens on the ground level, you can see the original stage and proscenium, and the original lilac and gold coloring. Bow Tie continues to operate this owned property in 2019.

Washington Township Cinemas, 249 Pascack Rd., Washington Twp., NJ
Cary Grant was first to grace the screen at this theater in *Walk, Don't Run*, on September 2, 1966. Anchoring a shopping center, the auditorium originally sat 650 in a wide auditorium. An independent divided it into three screens in 1980, and Clearview eventually took over. Bow Tie Cinemas lease ran out in September 2016, and the theater was closed for two months until another independent reopened it.

Wayne Preakness Cinemas, 1220 Hamburg Turnpike, Wayne, NJ
Architect Drew Eberson designed this shopping center theater which opened in May of 1964. Subsequently taken over by United Artists, the house was twinned and two more screens were added bringing it to a quadplex. Bow Tie operated it until September 2019, and an independent operator assumed the lease.

Anthony Wayne 5, 190 W. Lancaster Ave., Wayne, PA
The film *Old San Francisco* opened the art deco Anthony Wayne on Philadelphia's Main Line suburb of Wayne. Patrons entered through a mirrored entrance into a large foyer which had large artificial fountains on each side. The 1,318-seat auditorium featured a pipe organ and plush seating. A series of operators over the years divided the auditorium. Clearview split it into five, with one housed in the former stage house. Bow Tie only operated this location for two months before subletting it to a local operator.

Bala Theatre, 157 Bala Ave., Bala Cynwyd, PA
Noted Philadelphia architects Hoffman & Henon designed the 1,450-seat Egyptian for the Main Line town of Bala Cynwyd. Warner Brothers was the first operator of the Egyptian Revival–themed palace, the lobby of which features a mural of Cleopatra and her attendants. The rest rooms featured heavily furnished lounges. The large auditorium was split into three in 1994. At that time the balcony was sealed off and the projection booth was moved to that level. The original booth is abandoned above. Bow Tie operated this location for two months, spinning it off to a local operator in early August 2013.

Paris Theater, 4 W. 54th St., New York, NY
On November 6, 2019, Bow Tie reopened Manhattan's beloved single-screen Paris Theater on behalf of Marlene Dietrich cutting the ribbon. Netflix premiered their title *Marriage Story*, directed by Brooklyn native Noah Baumbach, there on November 10, 2019.

B.S. Moss Theatres has been involved with many partnerships over the years. These include a West Coast partnership with the Forman family, owners of Pacific Theaters. One of those co-operated locations was the Vine Theater on Hollywood Boulevard.

Rockland County, NY, also had three drive-in locations: the 303 Drive-In (Orangeburg, NY), Rockand Drive-In (Monsey, NY), and Nyack Drive-In (Blauvelt, NY), which were operated in the 1960s and 1970s by United Artists and B.S. Moss.

Several operational partnerships took place in Manhattan over the years, most notably in Times Square. With the Elson family, Moss operated the Embassy Newsreel Theater and the Forum Theater. Other deals with the Brandt family brought more locations into the fold.

Carried by such a rich history, the company continued into 2020, celebrating its 120th year in business. New experiences, such as Bow Tie Ultimate, BTX-Bow Tie X-Treme, and luxurious upgraded operations will secure the company's future for many years to come. Bow Tie is the only theater chain still in operation encompassing all stages of motion picture and live entertainment, from the golden age of the penny arcade and nickelodeon to the vaudeville house, movie palace, shopping center theater, mall multiplex, free-standing megaplex, and the modern luxury theater.

ACKNOWLEDGMENTS

I AM ESPECIALLY GRATEFUL to my wife Ann Cook and the following colleagues and friends for their assistance and support of this project:

- Ann whose wonderful taste and sage advice made this book the quality volume that it is.
- Joe Masher and his astounding knowledge of the history and genealogy of the Moss theaters, as reflected in the appendix, gave this project its historical gravitas.
- Liz Wolfe, with her amazing organizational skills, was able to create a research structure out of the voluminous historic materials that were available.
- Michael Levine, whose persistence in urging the writing of this book made it happen.
- Ken Whyte, in addition to his role as editor of *Magic in the Dark*, educated me as to the publishing world.
- Jonathan Kay, my colleague, and researcher extraordinaire, whose diligence and attention to detail formed the foundation for this book.

—Charley Moss